AMERICA the BEAUTIFUL

NEW HAMPSHIRE

By Sylvia McNair

Consultants

William L. Taylor, Professor of History; Director, Institute for New Hampshire Studies, Plymouth State College

Maryann J. Lacasse, Elementary Facilitator, Rochester, New Hampshire

Robert L. Hillerich, Ph.D., Bowling Green State University, Bowling Green, Ohio

CHILDRENS PRESS®
CHICAGO

Sugar maple trees in the fall in central New Hampshire

Project Editor: Joan Downing
Associate Editor: Shari Joffe
Design Director: Margrit Fiddle
Typesetting: Graphic Connections, Inc.
Engraving: Liberty Photoengraving

Library of Congress Cataloging-in-Publication Data

McNair, Sylvia.
    America the beautiful. New Hampshire / by Sylvia
McNair.
        p.   cm.
    Includes index.
    Summary: An introduction to the geography,
history, economy, people, and interesting sites of the
Granite State.
    ISBN 0-516-00475-1
    1. New Hampshire—Juvenile literature.
[1. New Hampshire.] I. Title.
F34.3.M36 1991   91-540
974.2—dc20   CIP
                                             AC

A church and covered bridge near Stark

TABLE OF CONTENTS

Chapter 1
THE OLD MAN OF THE MOUNTAIN

THE OLD MAN OF THE MOUNTAIN

New Hampshire is a beautiful, verdant state. Its geography has shaped its history. Its shoreline and bays, teeming with fish, lured the first settlers. Its location helped create wealth for early merchants and shipbuilders. The woods and streams brought fur traders and lumbermen. Fertile river valleys enticed farmers. The same rivers gave early industries the power to run mills and factories.

Over the years, the serene beauty of New Hampshire's mountains and lakes has attracted visitors who come for a quiet summer vacation, an awe-inspiring drive through brilliant autumn foliage, or an exhilarating weekend of swooping down snow-covered slopes.

Sooner or later, most visitors to the Granite State go to see the Old Man of the Mountain. He's only a pile of rocks, from most viewpoints. But from just the right spot down below, a man's face can be seen in profile high up on the mountainside. It doesn't look very big, from down there, and it's certainly not a face anyone would call handsome.

Yet the Old Man of the Mountain has inspired storytellers and poets, painters and photographers. He has become the symbol of the New Hampshire character—resolute, steadfast, loyal, and fiercely independent. One can easily imagine the words of the New Hampshire motto reverberating down the mountainside from the lips of the Old Man himself: "Live free or die!"

Chapter 2

THE LAND

THE LAND

Glaciers once covered the northeastern United States. When they retreated from the region now known as New Hampshire, they left behind a hard, gray, granite rock called gneiss. The rock was covered with a thin layer of soil that was sandy and full of gravel. In most places, the soil was too thin to grow trees.

Gradually, over many millennia, the rock crumbled, soil and seeds were blown in or dropped by birds, and a loamy soil began to cover the bedrock. Today, about 84 percent of New Hampshire's land is covered with forest.

New Hampshire is a small state. At its longest distances, it measures 180 miles (290 kilometers) from north to south and 93 miles (150 kilometers) from east to west. Covering only 9,279 square miles (24,033 square kilometers), it ranks forty-fourth among the states in land area.

Shaped roughly like a right triangle, New Hampshire is bordered on the east by Maine and the Atlantic Ocean, on the south by Massachusetts, on the west by Vermont and the Canadian province of Quebec, and on the north by Quebec. On a map, parts of these borders look as if they had been torn in ragged fashion instead of cut neatly with scissors along straight lines.

New Hampshire's eastern boundary with Maine runs straight south from the Canadian border until it reaches the Salmon Falls River. This river becomes the boundary line as it flows to the Piscataqua River and the Atlantic Ocean. At this point, New Hampshire has a tiny bit of seacoast, only 18 miles (29 kilometers) long. The state's southern boundary, with

New Hampshire's trademark stone walls were built by early farmers from the stones they gathered while clearing the rocky land.

Massachusetts, is uneven for a short stretch north of the Merrimack River, then proceeds west in a straight line to the Connecticut River. Most of the state's western border is determined by the Connecticut River. North of the Canadian border, New Hampshire's western boundary is formed by Halls Stream.

GEOGRAPHIC REGIONS

New Hampshire has three topographical regions: the Coastal Lowlands, the Eastern New England Upland, and the White Mountains.

The southeastern corner of the state, between the Atlantic Ocean and the Merrimack River Valley, is part of the New England region known as the Coastal Lowlands. The terrain

Farms in the Eastern New England Upland (above) produce such crops as apples (top right) and hay (bottom right).

consists of sandy beaches, salt marshes, and tidal inlets, as well as some meadowlands suitable for farming. Nine miles (14 kilometers) offshore are nine islands called the Isles of Shoals. The three southernmost of these are part of New Hampshire; the others belong to Maine. Marine life is plentiful in the ocean waters and inlets. Farmers in this region produce chickens, fruits, and nursery plants.

The Eastern New England Upland, which covers more than half the state, lies west and northwest of the Lowlands. This region is characterized by hills, river valleys, and hundreds of beautiful lakes. Some areas are marked by isolated hills of highly resistant rock, called monadnocks, that were left aboveground after erosion wore down the surrounding land. Two distinct valleys, separated by a spine of hills and mountains, are found in the region: the Merrimack Valley, on the east; and the Connecticut River Valley,

Winter at Franconia Ridge in the White Mountains

on the west. Where the ground is not too hilly, the soil of the New England Upland is deep and rich. Farms in the region produce hay, fruits, and dairy products. Granite, sand, gravel, and mica come from the region's quarries. New Hampshire's major industrial and population centers lie in the Merrimack Valley.

The White Mountains, part of the Appalachian mountain system, cover the northern third of the state. The best-known ranges of the White Mountains are the Presidential and Franconia ranges. The Presidential Range, which includes peaks named for United States presidents Washington, Adams, Jefferson, John Quincy Adams, Monroe, and Madison, boasts the highest elevations in New England. Mount Washington, the highest peak, rises to 6,288 feet (1,917 meters). New Hampshire's most famous natural landmark, the Old Man of the Mountain, is on Profile Mountain in Franconia Notch.

Squam Lake lies in central New Hampshire.

The White Mountains are appropriately named, not only because many peaks are snowcapped for much of the year, but because sunlight reflecting off rocky bluffs near the summits makes them look white even in summer.

RIVERS AND LAKES

New Hampshire has some 40,000 miles (64,372 kilometers) of waterways. The most important of its forty major rivers are the Connecticut, Merrimack, Saco, Androscoggin, and Piscataqua. The Connecticut River forms the state's western boundary from Quebec to Massachusetts and continues south to flow into Long Island Sound. The Merrimack rises south of the White Mountains and flows through the center of the state into Massachusetts, where it turns east to flow into the Atlantic Ocean. Its swift current has shaped New Hampshire's economy by furnishing waterpower for many factories. The Saco and Androscoggin rivers flow from northeastern New Hampshire into Maine, then empty

14

into the Atlantic. The Piscataqua runs along the southern part of the Maine border and forms a large bay at Portsmouth.

Many of the state's two thousand lakes and ponds are surrounded by summer homes and resorts. New Hampshire's largest body of water is Lake Winnipesaukee, located a few miles south of the White Mountains in the east-central part of the state. Covering 72 square miles (186 square kilometers), the lake is surrounded by three mountain ranges—Ossipee, Sandwich, and Belknap—and contains 274 islands. Other major lakes include Umbagog, Squam, Newfound, Winnisquam, Ossipee, and Sunapee.

PLANTS AND ANIMALS

New Hampshire is one of the nation's most densely wooded states; about five-sixths of the state is forest-covered. About two-thirds of the state's forests are made up of such evergreens as pines, spruces, firs, cedars, and tamaracks. Mixed hardwoods, including maples, beeches, birches, oaks, ashes, and hickories, account for about a third of the state's forest cover. The hills are covered with brightly colored foliage in autumn. In the spring, apple and cherry trees, as well as dogwood, azalea, honeysuckle, and rhododendron shrubs, produce a dazzling display of blooms.

Native mammals include opossums, moles, shrews, bats, porcupines, raccoons, muskrats, weasels, minks, skunks, chipmunks, foxes, squirrels, and rabbits. The Lake Umbagog area, which straddles the Maine border in northern New Hampshire, is home to an outstanding array of wildlife, including white-tailed deer, black bears, and even moose and elk, as well as such rare creatures as martens and Canada lynxes. Water birds nest here and migratory birds stop over in great numbers.

New Hampshire's wide array of wildlife includes martens (top left), seals (bottom left), and porcupines (right).

Along the seacoast and off the Isles of Shoals, Atlantic harbor seals, dolphins, and an occasional whale can be spotted. Birds commonly seen in the state include robins, chickadees, woodpeckers, blue jays, purple finches, whippoorwills, and sparrows, as well as ruffed grouse, pheasants, and ducks. Bass, landlocked salmon, pickerel, perch, whitefish, and several varieties of trout swim in New Hampshire's lakes and streams.

CLIMATE

New Hampshire's weather, like that of the other states in the far Northeast, is often harsh and challenging. Winters are long and cold; summers short, with warm days and cool evenings. Growing seasons range from fewer than 105 days in the far north to 120 to 140 days in the south and near the Connecticut River.

New Hampshire winters are usually long, cold, and snowy.

In the far north, the temperature on an average day in January or February is about 16 degrees Fahrenheit (minus 9 degrees Celsius). In the summer, temperatures in the north average about 66 degrees Fahrenheit (19 degrees Celsius). In the southern part of the state, average temperatures are several degrees higher in both summer and winter. The lowest temperature ever recorded in the state was minus 46 degrees Fahrenheit (minus 43 degrees Celsius). New Hampshire's highest recorded temperature was 106 degrees Fahrenheit (41 degrees Celsius).

Annual rainfall in the state averages from 30 to 50 inches (76 to 127 centimeters). Yearly snowfall averages about 50 inches (127 centimeters) along the coast and as much as 150 inches (381 centimeters) in the mountains.

Records of temperature and wind velocity are kept at an observatory on the top of Mount Washington. The highest wind velocity ever recorded on earth—231 miles per hour (372 kilometers per hour)—was measured there on April 12, 1934.

Chapter 3
THE PEOPLE

THE PEOPLE

Daniel Webster, one of New Hampshire's most famous sons, is said to have made this comment about the rock formation known as the Old Man of the Mountain: "Men hang out their signs indicative of their respective trades: shoemakers hang out a gigantic shoe; jewelers a monster watch . . . but up in the mountains of New Hampshire, God Almighty has hung out a sign to show that here He makes men."

New Hampshirites are proud of this quotation. They feel it implies something good about the character of the state's people — that they are rock-solid, independent, courageous, and undaunted by the rigors of the harsh New Hampshire climate. They'll tell you that their people are hardworking, honest, frugal, and conservative.

Of course, it is dangerous to make generalizations about people of a certain region, especially in a time when many people move a half-dozen times in a lifetime. But symbols of good character are worth revering, and the Old Man is one the people of New Hampshire love dearly.

POPULATION GROWTH AND DISTRIBUTION

New Hampshire is one of the smallest states in terms of population. The nation's earliest census, in 1790, counted 141,885 residents in New Hampshire. Over the next fifty years, this number doubled. Then growth slowed down, as many of the state's young people left to start new communities on America's

A 4-H Club competition at the Deerfield Fair

frontier. By 1850, all of the Great Lakes states—Ohio, Indiana, Illinois, Michigan, Wisconsin, and Minnesota—had many settlers who had come from New Hampshire. The gold rush in California and other prospects drew New Hampshirites to the West Coast as well.

By 1950, New Hampshire's population was not quite double that of 1840, but since then, many newcomers have made their homes in New Hampshire. According to the 1980 census, New Hampshire had 920,610 people, ranking it forty-second in population among the states. Preliminary 1990 census figures, however, indicate that the state's population has surpassed 1 million, changing the state's rank to fortieth in population.

Much of New Hampshire is still rural; only a little more than half the people live in cities and towns. The largest cities are

Above: Picnickers in the White Mountains
Right: Ice fishing on Bradley Lake

concentrated in the southern part of the state; two thirds of New Hampshire's residents live in this region. Manchester is the state's most populous city, followed by Nashua, Concord (the state capital), Portsmouth, Salem, Dover, and Keene.

NEW HAMPSHIRE'S ETHNIC HERITAGE

Piscataqua, Sunapee, Winnipesaukee, Winnisquam, Ossipee, Umbagog—these and many other New Hampshire place names are the legacy of the Native Americans (American Indians) who lived in the region when the first European settlers arrived. These people, known as the western Abenaki, belonged to the eastern branch of the Algonquian language family, a large group of tribes related by similar languages and customs. Though most of the Indians left the region by the late 1700s, their early presence in New Hampshire contributed much to the state's character.

New Hampshire's forests, wildlife, and seacoast were responsible for bringing in the first European colonists. They were attracted by the abundance of fish and lobsters in the ocean and the fur-bearing animals and fine timber in the forests. A favorite New Hampshire story tells of a Boston preacher who came to Dover in the late 1600s. While giving a sermon, he urged his listeners to be faithful to "the divine purpose for which this colony was planted," only to be interrupted by a New Hampshire voice that declared, "Parson, we came hither to fish."

Most of New Hampshire's earliest settlers were English or of English descent. Even today, people think of the "typical" New Hampshire native as being a "Yankee" descended from Protestant English or Scottish colonists. In the 1990s, about half the state's residents fit that description.

The development of industry in southern New Hampshire during the first half of the nineteenth century was responsible for several waves of immigration. Posters displayed in England and Scotland advertised jobs in Manchester's Amoskeag textile mills, promising good wages for spinners, weavers, and dyers.

Irish immigrants were the first Europeans other than the English and the Scottish to come to New Hampshire in great numbers. First arriving in the 1840s, their numbers swelled in the 1850s after a great potato famine in Ireland starved them out.

Meanwhile, the French-speaking Canadian province of Quebec, which bordered New Hampshire on the north, was having trouble supporting its fast-growing population. Many French Canadians began to move to New England during the second half of the nineteenth century. By 1900, about 18 percent of New Hampshire's people were of Quebec origin. Today, about one-fourth of the state's people are of French-Canadian descent.

Many of the earliest French Canadians came to work in the

textile centers; others cut wood in the northern lumber camps or became brick makers. The newcomers quickly established French-language churches, newspapers in French, and French Catholic schools. At first, the French Canadians formed tight-knit communities that were called *petit Canadas* (little Canadas). This kept them out of the mainstream of New Hampshire politics for a time. But by the turn of the century, French Canadians who had become bilingual and bicultural began to gain political influence.

The late 1800s also saw an influx of German, Italian, Polish, and Greek immigrants, as well as smaller numbers of people from Norway, Sweden, Finland, and Russia.

Today, only about 4 percent of the state's residents are foreign-born; the national average is 6 percent. Ten percent of the population speak a language other than English at home, and more than sixty thousand people claim French as their first language. About 98 percent of the state's residents are white, a far greater proportion than the national average of 83 percent. African Americans make up less than 1 percent of the population.

RELIGION AND POLITICS

New Hampshire was overwhelmingly Protestant during its colonial and early statehood days. In fact, until 1819, Congregationalism was virtually the official religion of New Hampshire—all residents were taxed to support the Congregational church. Gradually, other Protestant denominations, including the Baptist, Presbyterian, Quaker, and Anglican churches, began to appear. In the second half of the nineteenth century, as the state's population became ethnically diverse, Roman Catholic, Greek Orthodox, Russian Orthodox, and Jewish congregations were established. However, non-Protestants

Towns throughout the state hold festivals that celebrate New Hampshire's varied ethnic heritage.

were barred from holding state public office until 1877. The word *Protestant* was even used in the state's Bill of Rights; it was not removed from that document until 1902.

Today, most New Hampshirites belong to one of the Protestant denominations, though Roman Catholics make up the largest single religious denomination. The leading Protestant churches in the state are the United Church of Christ, United Methodist, and American Baptist.

Politically, New Hampshire has long been considered a conservative state. The Republican party has been able to count on New Hampshire in almost every presidential election since 1945. In state and local offices, however, Democrats and Republicans are more evenly represented. In 1985, 33 percent of New Hampshire's state legislators were women, the highest percentage of any state.

Chapter 4
THE BEGINNING

THE BEGINNING

Fish, furs, and forests: these three valuable natural resources drew European settlers to the shores of New England. Early explorers of the Atlantic region—John Cabot of England, Giovanni da Verrazano of Italy, and Samuel de Champlain of France—brought back reports of islands and a mainland covered with thick forests.

By the late 1500s, fishermen from several European nations were reaping a bountiful harvest from the waters along the shores from present-day Massachusetts to Newfoundland. Temporary fishing bases were established on the islands years before there were any permanent settlements on the mainland. For some time there was no interest in settling or farming the territory, only in fishing and trading for furs with the Native Americans.

Kings of both England and France claimed the land that was to become New Hampshire. In 1605, Samuel de Champlain of France visited the New Hampshire coast. Over the next few years, he mapped the coasts of Maine, New Hampshire, and Massachusetts, including the inlets, harbors, headlands, and islands.

A few years later, English captain John Smith was hired to explore and map the same territory for the Northern Virginia Company, which was backed by English investors. He published a description of the area, which he named New England. In his account, the Isles of Shoals—which he named Smith's Islands—were described as rocky islands that appeared desolate and barren but were "furnished with good woods, springs, fruits, fish, and fowl."

Captain John Smith of England explored the Isles of Shoals, which he named Smith's Islands, in 1614.

FIRST EUROPEAN SETTLERS

In 1620, a stock company called the Council for New England was formed in England. A charter from England's King James I gave the council authority to issue land grants in the New World. Those early land grants often described property lines in vague terms based on poor information about the geography. Disputes over conflicting claims were common during the colonial period.

One such grant—a huge, imprecisely defined piece of land in present-day New Hampshire and Maine—was given to English merchants John Mason and Sir Ferdinando Gorges in 1622. Wishing to establish colonies in the region, Mason sent several groups across the Atlantic. The founder of the first settlement in what would become the state of New Hampshire was a Scotsman, David Thomson. In 1623, he sailed from Plymouth, England, with a small group of colonists. They landed at Odiorne's Point in what is now the town of Rye, found a supply of fresh water, and built homes, fishing camps, and a saltworks for preserving fish. They named their settlement Pannaway Plantation.

The Piscataqua harbor, where five fingers of land point into a 24-square-mile (62-square-kilometer) natural basin, was an ideal place to start a settlement. Four towns were established in the colony by 1640, all within a few miles of the seacoast and the Piscataqua River. They were Hilton's Point, now Dover; Strawbery Banke, which later became Portsmouth; and, to the south, Exeter and Hampton, founded by clergymen from the Massachusetts colony. By that time, nearly a thousand people lived in the vicinity.

In 1629, Gorges and Mason agreed to divide their land holdings. Mason named his portion—the land that lay between the Merrimack and Piscataqua rivers—in honor of his home county of Hampshire, England. He never laid eyes on New Hampshire, however, for he died without ever coming to America.

The attitudes and goals of the first New Hampshire colonists were quite different from those who settled the Plymouth and Massachusetts Bay colonies. For the most part, the New Hampshire colonists were motivated not by a desire for religious freedom—they came to seek their fortunes.

In 1641, the four New Hampshire towns, unable to form a system of centralized government agreeable to all, put themselves under the jurisdiction of the Massachusetts Bay Colony. New Hampshire remained a part of Massachusetts until 1679, when England's King Charles II made it a separate royal province.

FISHING, FARMING, AND FUR TRAPPING

Most of the early settlers of the New World were farmers, or at least grew some of their own food. But several other occupations were particularly important to the growth of the New Hampshire region.

The volume of fish caught in New Hampshire waters was never as great as the large quantities netted off the shores of Massachusetts and Newfoundland. Fishing was, nevertheless, a mainstay of the colony's economy for a long time. People back in England were eager to buy all the fish the colonists could supply.

Fur trading, on the other hand, was not as successful as the traders and investors originally had hoped. For a number of years, beaver pelts were much sought after, because hats made of beaver fur were all the rage in Europe. Both European trappers and the Native Americans with whom they traded hunted and killed beavers until they were nearly wiped out. At about that time, fashions changed and the Europeans no longer wanted large quantities of beaver fur. By the end of the 1600s, the fur trade was virtually dead.

Beavers had, however, left their mark on the land, and the dams they built affected the way the colony developed. The dams became bridges; the ponds created by the dams were used as sites for mills. Then, as the beaver population dwindled, dams crumbled and the waters behind them flowed away. Acres of thick, rich loam were laid bare. Farmers were delighted to find land ready for planting, with no trees and brush to be cleared away.

LUMBERING

Before long, New Hampshire's early settlers discovered that their most valuable asset was the vast virgin forest that seemed to stretch on forever. Wood supplied a great many of the colonists' needs. It was used to build, heat, and furnish houses. Most containers and many tools were made of wood. People did not yet use petroleum for energy and heat. They had no steel, no plastics,

Fur trading in New England in the 1600s

no electricity. They depended on wood for many of the necessities of life. It is easy to see why wood was so important to a young, developing country. Wood was also in great demand in other parts of the world. England's forests were nearly gone; they had been overused for centuries.

By the 1630s, sawmills appeared, often beside beaver ponds, to convert timber into lumber. A brisk trade quickly developed. Ships loaded with wood and fish sailed from Portsmouth to England, southern Europe, and the West Indies. They came back from the Caribbean filled with things the colonists needed—corn, fruits and nuts, cotton, indigo, and tobacco.

New Hampshire's white pines had a special significance in those days. They were tall, straight, and nearly free of branches except at the top. Some of them grew to be giants, 150-to-200-feet (46-to-61-meters) tall and 3 feet (1 meter) or more in diameter. They were called "mast pines" because they were greatly prized as

31

In the seventeenth century, logs from New Hampshire's vast pine forests began being used as masts for English ships.

masts for ships. The English navy looked all over the world for trees like these, and the ones growing in New Hampshire were among the finest to be found. Masts were often damaged in battle, so there was a constant demand for the trees. New Hampshire masts lasted much longer than those made from Norwegian trees.

Imagine how difficult it was to transport these huge masts to market! The logs were usually carried to the port in winter, when they could be loaded on sleds and pulled across the snow-covered land. As many as eighty oxen were hitched to sleds filled with the enormous, priceless cargo. Heavy ships were specially designed and built to carry the masts across the ocean.

The English government tried to make sure that the best mast pines would be reserved for the English navy. All trees not on private property and over a certain size were declared to be the property of the Crown. Deputies roamed the forests, marking such trees by cutting an arrowlike sign into the trunk with an ax.

Although the punishment for cutting the king's trees was

severe, many colonists nevertheless defied the orders. They wanted to use the logs themselves or saw them into boards—much easier to transport than huge heavy logs—for export.

Merchants and others grew wealthy from the lumber trade. As the forests near the coast were cut down, inland settlements began to appear. A lively land speculation developed as people came to fill the jobs created by the lumber industry. Lumberers, sawyers, coopers (barrel-makers), and carpenters found work in New Hampshire's new communities. In the port cities, shipwrights, sailmakers, and mariners were in demand.

THE FRENCH AND INDIAN WARS

For seventy-four years, from 1689 to 1763, two European nations competed for control of North American lands. Traders and trappers from France came to find valuable furs to sell in Europe. They wanted to build trading outposts and deal with the Native Americans. For the most part, they got along quite well with the Native Americans.

People from England came for a different reason. They wanted to build settlements where they could live permanently. The Native Americans did not understand this. They believed that land belonged to everyone, not to individuals. At first, they were friendly to the newcomers, but as their lands were taken over and turned into farms and villages, their attitudes changed.

England and France fought four separate wars during this period. Together, these conflicts became known as the French and Indian Wars. For the most part, Native Americans sided with the French. None of the major battles of these wars took place on New Hampshire soil, but many New Hampshirites fought for the English side, and a number of Indian raids in New Hampshire made life dangerous in the colony. Two New Hampshire men, Robert Rogers and John Stark, particularly distinguished themselves as military leaders during the wars. England and France signed a peace treaty in 1763, and life grew more pleasant and prosperous in the New Hampshire colony. But peace in the colonies was not to last for very long.

A COLONIAL DYNASTY

The Wentworths were New Hampshire's most influential family throughout much of the 1700s. They played starring roles in the colony's political, economic, and social life.

In 1717, the king of England appointed John Wentworth, a wealthy, self-made merchant, lieutenant governor of New Hampshire. At the time, a single royal governor administered both Massachusetts and New Hampshire.

Wentworth was a gifted administrator and politician. He strengthened the legal system of the colony and made the system of taxation fairer. He knew how to compromise and at the same time increase his own power. He also made sure that his own family gained many political and economic advantages—as did most politicians of his day.

Even in the early 1700s, some New Hampshirites were growing uneasy about England's control over them, but Wentworth saw Massachusetts as an even greater threat. The boundary line between the two colonies was not clear. Massachusetts tried to claim the southern New Hampshire towns. Both Wentworth and the Massachusetts governor began granting charters to towns within the area under dispute. Some people criticized Wentworth for giving most of these charters to his own, wealthy friends. He reasoned that it took capital to get a new town started.

An engraving of Benning Wentworth's house near New Castle

John Wentworth died in 1730. Jonathan Belcher, the royal governor of Massachusetts and a Wentworth opponent, took over the administration of New Hampshire for a few years.

John Wentworth's son Benning, along with other supporters, worked to separate New Hampshire and Massachusetts. In 1740, the king's Privy Council estabished a boundary that gave New Hampshire 3,500 square miles (9,065 square kilometers) of land and twenty-eight towns that had been claimed by the Massachusetts Bay Colony. The next year, the king chose Benning Wentworth as the first independent governor of the province of New Hampshire.

BENNING WENTWORTH

Benning Wentworth served as a royal governor longer than any other governor in the American colonies. He was a loyal supporter of the Crown and of the Anglican church. The English government protected its loyal colonists and was particularly interested in keeping control of the province that was furnishing the valuable masts for the navy.

Partly to expand his political base, and partly for profit, Benning Wentworth began an active program of granting lands for new settlement and development. All in all, he made some two hundred land grants in New Hampshire, including seventy-five townships. In most cases, he reserved several hundred acres in each new township for himself. His holdings grew to more than 100,000 acres (40,469 hectares).

Claiming that New Hampshire's territory extended west as far as Lake Champlain, Benning Wentworth granted charters for more than a hundred townships west of the Connecticut River. The first of these townships he named Bennington—after himself. But this area, now the state of Vermont, was also claimed by New York. In 1764, the British Crown settled the dispute in New York's favor, and New Hampshire's western boundary was set along the west bank of the Connecticut River. Even so, until the founding of Vermont in 1777, the area west of the river was known as the New Hampshire Grants.

The Wentworth family grew more and more wealthy and powerful while Benning was governor. Benning's brother Mark made a fortune through acquiring masts for the royal navy. The colony thrived too, growing prosperous and strong under Benning's leadership. Roads were built and stagecoaches began regular service between Portsmouth and Boston.

In the 1760s, Britain imposed one tax after another on the American colonists. In 1765, the British Parliament passed the Stamp Act, which required the colonists to buy tax stamps for legal documents and newspapers. This new tax made the colonists particularly angry. They resented being taxed while not being allowed to send representatives to Parliament.

New Hampshirites shared the growing indignation of other colonists over Britain's tyranny. In Portsmouth, the colonists hung

Indignant over the passage of the Stamp Act, American colonists, including some New Hampshirites, vented their anger by attacking the officials sent to distribute the stamps.

effigies (dummies) of the tax official who had been sent by the British to distribute the stamps.

Benning Wentworth had been a good governor and was well liked, but as a representative of the Crown, he became a target of general resentment. In failing health, he resigned from office in 1766. The new royal appointee was young John Wentworth, son of Benning's brother Mark.

THE LAST ROYAL GOVERNOR

New Hampshire now had about fifty-three thousand residents, most of whom lived in one of three small areas—the east coast, the Merrimack Valley, and the Connecticut Valley. Governor John Wentworth was more interested than his uncle and grandfather had been in developing the interior of the state. He traveled a great deal, surveying the forests for mast trees and observing the lives of woodsmen. He developed a plantation on Lake Winnipesaukee, where he studied wildlife and agriculture.

Governor Wentworth initiated the division of the province into counties, so that residents would not have to travel so far to conduct legal transactions. He also called for the building of much-needed roads into the colony's interior. The new road system helped connect isolated settlements and brought more trade into New Hampshire.

In 1769, Governor Wentworth gave 40,000 acres (16,188 hectares) of land in Hanover to Reverend Eleazar Wheelock on which to build a school to educate both Indians and young colonists. Wheelock offered to name the new school in honor of the governor. Wentworth declined the honor, asking instead that it be named for the Earl of Dartmouth, an English lord whose favor he was courting. Provincial leaders soon looked to Dartmouth College to educate ministers to serve New England parishes. Dartmouth College eventually became one of New England's great institutions of higher learning.

REVOLUTIONARY TIMES

A revolutionary spirit was growing in New Hampshire, as it was in the other colonies. Even though New Hampshire was prospering under its royal governors, many residents were anxious to join hands with their neighbors in protesting excess taxation and repressive laws issued from England.

Governor Wentworth tried to hold back the tide of opposition to the Crown. Twice he dissolved the New Hampshire Assembly and called for new elections. But control over the province was slipping out of his hands, and the more radical assembly was gaining power. Several meetings were held in which people talked of revolution.

When Wentworth dissolved the assembly in 1774, the colonists

Dartmouth College in 1803

took matters into their own hands. A call was sent out asking each town to elect a representative to a New Hampshire provincial congress that would meet in Exeter. This congress chose two representatives to represent New Hampshire at the First Continental Congress, to be held in Philadelphia in September.

In December, four hundred New Hampshire men stormed the British fort at New Castle, near Portsmouth. They carried off arms and ammunition and distributed them among the inland towns. Many historians consider this to be the first warlike act of the American Revolution. Wentworth tried to maintain control over the provincial militia, but when fighting broke out the next spring in Lexington and Concord, Massachusetts, hundreds of New Hampshire militiamen hurried to Massachusetts to join the other colonists in resisting the British redcoats.

In June 1775, forced from office, the governor packed up his family and moved into a British fort at New Castle. In August, they left New Hampshire, never to return. They moved to the British colony of Nova Scotia, Canada, where Wentworth was later appointed royal governor. So ended 160 years of colonial government in New Hampshire.

Chapter 5

A NEW STATE, NEW PATHS

A NEW STATE, NEW PATHS

Even before the flight of the royal governor, the people of New Hampshire had taken several steps toward independence. In May 1775, the Provincial Congress of New Hampshire had set up a revolutionary government. This government called for three New Hampshire regiments to join the other colonies in fighting the British, and levied a tax to support them. A Committee of Safety was appointed to administer the province.

In January 1776, New Hampshire became the first of the thirteen colonies to adopt a state constitution. On June 15, New Hampshire lawmakers adopted the New Hampshire Declaration of Independence, which instructed New Hampshire's delegates to the Continental Congress to vote for freeing the colonies from Britain. Three weeks later, on July 4, New Hampshire's delegates joined those of the other thirteen colonies in signing the national Declaration of Independence.

Official papers and proclamations issued by New Hampshire's new revolutionary government used words that carried an important symbolic message about the shift in power. Documents from the office of the royal governor and the colonial government had always ended with the words "God Save the King." The new government substituted the words "God Save the People."

THE REVOLUTIONARY WAR

New Hampshire was represented in every important battle of the Revolutionary War, from Bunker Hill to the British surrender

During the Revolutionary War, Portsmouth produced a special type of workboat called a *gundalow*.

at Yorktown. About four thousand of the state's men fought with the Continental army, some for the entire duration of the war. Those at home did not have to suffer invasion; New Hampshire was the only one of the original thirteen states where no battles were fought.

Initially, the war was hard on Portsmouth. The seat of government had moved to Exeter, and revenues from shipping and trade were down. Two other activities, however, helped to make up for these losses: shipbuilding and privateering.

Some three thousand New Hampshirites served the revolutionary cause by privateering. They cruised the waters from Nova Scotia to the West Indies in armed ships, capturing unarmed British merchant ships and supply ships and seizing their cargoes for the Continental army.

Shipbuilding had been growing in importance in the Piscataqua region for nearly a century before the Revolution. It was a natural outgrowth of lumbering and shipping, a link between the two industries. Three naval vessels were constructed in the shipyards at Portsmouth for use during the war. A special type of boat built in the area, called a *gundalow*, was used as a workboat. The gundalow was a long, low, freight barge with a triangular sail hung on a long spar from a low mast. Its design was ideal for carrying heavy loads through inland waters.

The shipbuilding industry thrived after the Revolution. Portsmouth builders could produce a ship at a much lower cost than could European craftsmen. This was the era of magnificent, heavy clipper ships, and between 1800 and 1850, nearly five hundred ships were built in Portsmouth shipyards.

REGIONALISM

In the 1770s, most of New Hampshire's residents lived in one of three areas: in the Piscataqua area, where Portsmouth and Exeter are located; in the southern part of the state, or along the Connecticut River. The northern section, up in the White Mountains, had very few inhabitants.

Portsmouth, home of the royal governor, had been the social, political, and economic center from the beginning. The leaders of New Hampshire society lived like aristocrats, in fine houses with servants. For the most part, these people were more conservative—more loyal to England and to the Anglican church—than people living elsewhere in New Hampshire.

The people of Exeter, in contrast, felt a greater degree of dissatisfaction with England's treatment of the colonies. In Exeter, the elected assembly had more influence than did the governor and his council. The seat of government was moved from Portsmouth to Exeter after the governor fled, and political power was never concentrated in Portsmouth again.

The southern towns were settled by people from Massachusetts, and their ties with that colony remained strong. Farming was the major pursuit in this region.

The third region consisted of the towns in western New Hampshire along the east side of the Connecticut River. Most of the pioneers in this region had come from Connecticut to farm. The area's major trade route was the Connecticut River, not the ocean, and the residents had few ties with either England or Massachusetts. In fact, their closest ties were with the towns on the west side of the river that were known as the New Hampshire Grants.

The people of New Hampshire's Connecticut River towns were not satisfied with the state constitution of 1776. They felt that they did not have enough representation in the New Hampshire Assembly, and that more power should be in the hands of the towns, rather than the state.

Calling itself Vermont, the area known as the New Hampshire Grants declared itself an independent republic in 1777. Soon after, thirty-six disgruntled towns on the east side of the Connecticut River temporarily seceded from New Hampshire and joined Vermont. In 1782, under pressure from President George Washington, the western towns rejoined New Hampshire. Even so, the secession had not been without results. New Hampshire's legislature, recognizing that it needed the support of the valuable Connecticut River townships, set about providing a state constitution more acceptable to the western region.

NEW CONSTITUTIONS

First to adopt its own constitution, New Hampshire was also the first of the original thirteen states to call a convention to write a better one. It was agreed that the new constitution would be submitted to the voters for ratification. It took three tries before the voters accepted a document. Finally, in 1784, a new constitution was adopted.

The new state constitution gave the western towns broader representation. Today, the state assembly, whose official name is the general court, has more members than any other state legislature. Its size demonstrates New Hampshire's firm belief, handed down through the centuries, in grass-roots democracy.

Meanwhile, representatives from all the states were laboring over a constitution for the new United States of America. It would be adopted when nine states, two-thirds of the total, ratified it. On June 21, 1788, New Hampshire's vote carried the day, and the United States Constitution became the law of the land.

Later, political and economic power shifted to the Merrimack Valley region. In 1808, it was decided that the seat of government would be moved to Concord, and construction of a capitol building began there in 1814. In 1819, the legislature met for the first time in the new State House, a lovely building constructed of New Hampshire granite and trimmed with Vermont marble.

The growth of manufacturing and the birth of the industrial revolution soon made Manchester, downriver from Concord, the economic center of the state.

THE FAMILY FARM

Most early settlers in the American colonies were farmers, at least part-time. Even though fishing, fur trading, lumbering, shipping, and shipbuilding were the main sources of income in early New Hampshire, most families raised a large portion of their own food.

Before planting could begin, New Hampshire's rugged land had to be cleared of rocks and boulders.

However, New Hampshire's land was not ideal for farming. Most of it was covered with forest or brush. The soil was rocky, the growing season short. Europeans who came to this land brought with them the philosophy that man should tame nature, should fight and defeat the wilderness. They did not look at nature as something to live with and adapt to, as did the Native Americans.

Each family tried to be as self-sufficient as possible. They grew crops for food and raised livestock for hides and wool, as well as for meat and milk. If times were good, they would have some surplus to take to market to exchange for the products they could not raise or make for themselves.

Industrious and hardworking men and women cleared the forested hills and valleys of southern New Hampshire, removed the rocks and boulders, laid out roads, built stone-wall fences, and planted crops. They grew some of the same things the Native Americans had grown—corn, beans, squash, and pumpkins. They also planted seeds brought from Europe, to grow wheat, barley, oats, rye, and hay. Later European immigrants brought in apples and potatoes.

The wealthy merchants along the coast suffered severe losses of income during the Revolution, but the farmers did well. Their products were needed to keep the army fed.

Nearly all the land in New Hampshire, except that in the far northern third of the state, was under cultivation by the early 1800s. As the century progressed, young people began to move out. Young men left New Hampshire, lured by cheap land in the West; young women went to work in mills in southern New Hampshire and in Massachusetts.

Gradually the type of farming changed, as well. The small landholdings in New Hampshire could not compete with large midwestern farmlands and western ranches in producing grains, meat, and wool. By the end of the nineteenth century, New Hampshire's major farm products were fruits, potatoes, poultry, and dairy products.

THE FACTORY

As towns were settled in New Hampshire, the first commercial buildings to appear were mills—sawmills to process lumber and gristmills to grind grain. Water was the source of power used to run the saws and millstones.

Early manufacturing took place at home. Linen cloth of fine quality was made by hand in the Merrimack Valley long before the area developed into one of the world's leading textile centers.

Individual families grew the flax, carded it, spun the thread, and wove the cloth by hand. Linen from Londonderry was sold to far-off markets in the early 1700s.

The manufacture of cloth began shifting from the home to small factories in the early 1800s. The state's first factory for making cotton cloth opened in New Ipswich in 1803. In Manchester, the Amoskeag Mills introduced a power loom for weaving cloth in 1819.

In 1831, the Amoskeag Mills were reincorporated as the Amoskeag Manufacturing Company, with $1 million in new capital. By this time, about forty cotton mills and more than fifty woolen-carding mills operated in the state, but the Amoskeag company would soon become the giant of New Hampshire's textile industry. As it grew, the Amoskeag company expanded into heavy construction and engineering. It built much of its own power machinery as well as its mills and power plants. It also built a model city for its workers, complete with housing, schools, churches, and parks. This "company town" of Manchester eventually grew to be the state's largest city.

The owners of textile mills in New Hampshire and Massachusetts started out with high-minded ideals. They were paternalistic, meaning that, like a father, they had far-reaching plans for their factories, towns, and employees. The companies provided not only housing, but also recreational opportunities and cultural events such as lectures and concerts. From rural areas, the companies recruited families, single men, and single women to work in the factories. The mill workers labored long hours under hazardous conditions, but most felt that their jobs provided a greater opportunity than life on the family farm.

In the mid-1800s, the companies began looking for cheaper labor abroad. A severe potato famine in Ireland brought a wave of

The Amoskeag Manufacturing Company, which began as a cotton mill, eventually expanded into a variety of other enterprises, such as the manufacture of steam fire engines.

Irish immigrants to America. The textile mills offered these desperate people new opportunities. The mills hired large numbers of German, Swedish, Scottish, Greek, Polish, and—most of all—French-Canadian immigrants. Whole families worked in the factories; there were no laws against child labor until 1914. Despite the low wages and difficult working conditions, the workers were glad to come. Times were even harder in their native countries. By 1900, two of every five people in New Hampshire were either foreign-born or had a parent who had been born in another country.

The Amoskeag company expanded its paternalistic services as the makeup of its labor force changed. Classes in cooking, gardening, sewing, and English were offered for the new immigrants. The company built playgrounds and provided health services and loans for home mortgages. Since Amoskeag employed more than two-thirds of Manchester's residents, the company's influence on politics was immense.

The Abbot-Downing
company produced
the world-famous
Concord coach.

The state's first shoe factory opened in 1823, and by the early
1900s, the dollar value of shoes produced in New Hampshire was
even greater than that of textiles.

TRANSPORTATION

A toll road, or turnpike, as such roads were then called, was
built between Portsmouth and Concord in 1795. Many roads
followed during the nineteenth century, both in New Hampshire
and across the nation, as Americans moved west.

In Concord, the wagon manufacturer that became the Abbot-
Downing Company began making springless buggies in 1813. The
company became famous for its Concord coach, the best coach of
its kind. It had leather padding that acted as a shock absorber and
provided a more comfortable ride than that of other coaches of its
time. Throughout much of the 1800s, the sturdy Concord coach
was the principal mode of transportation for United States mail
carriers and families migrating to the West. Records show that in
1890, the company produced about two thousand coaches,
carriages, and wagons that were sold throughout the world.

Canals were built and used for a few years as waterways for freight, but after 1850, railroads became the most important means of transportation in New Hampshire. More than two hundred locomotives, the "iron horses" used to pull the trains, were built by the Amoskeag Manufacturing Company of Manchester. The Laconia Car Shops, established in 1859, became famous manufacturers of railroad cars.

Railroads linked small, isolated towns to the outside world. Trains carried fresh milk, eggs, and other farm products to market rapidly, and brought in factory-made goods that had previously been difficult to get. Farmers began to alter their production to grow more cash crops for sale in the cities.

Railroad owners became the most powerful political force in the state. They used free passes for political purposes, giving them out generously to such influential people as newspaper editors and lawyers. The political influence of the railroads grew as the farmers and merchants became more dependent on them. Legislators knew that voting against the railroad interests might result in the closing of the local depot or a sudden increase in shipping fees.

NEW HAMPSHIRITES IN WASHINGTON

Daniel Webster is perhaps New Hampshire's most famous son. He was born in 1782 in Salisbury and graduated from Dartmouth College. He was a representative from New Hampshire in the United States Congress from 1813 to 1817. After moving to Massachusetts, he returned to Washington, serving in both the House of Representatives and in the Senate. He served as United States secretary of state under three presidents.

Webster is best remembered as a gifted speaker. In one of his famous cases, he represented Dartmouth College when the New Hampshire legislature tried to take over its management and turn it into a state university. Webster won the case for the college in an argument before the United States Supreme Court.

By the middle of the 1800s, the nation was becoming increasingly divided over the question of slavery. A two-year war with Mexico, ending in 1848, had added more than 500,000 square miles (1.3 million square kilometers) of western territory to the United States. A bitter argument over whether or not slavery would be permitted in the new states to be created from the territory was dividing people in the North and South.

Daniel Webster was one of the senators who worked out and passed the Compromise of 1850, which helped delay the outbreak of the Civil War for a few years. The compromise admitted California as a free state, which pleased the North. To appease the South, a new and strict Fugitive Slave Law was passed, making it a federal offense to help runaway slaves.

Two years later, at the national convention of the Democratic party, New Hampshirite Franklin Pierce was selected to run for the presidency of the United States. The Democratic party—made up of both northerners and southerners—was, like the nation as a whole, divided over the issue of slavery. Pierce appeased both sides and won the nomination by taking the position that although slavery was indeed wrong, its future in the states where it already existed should be determined only by the people of those states.

Pierce won a resounding victory in the national election. Yet the problems facing the nation during this period were too much for the president to solve. He could not bring the conflicting factions together, and he was not renominated for a second term.

Another native of New Hampshire, Salmon P. Chase, was a

President Franklin Pierce (left) and famed orator and statesman Daniel Webster (above) both hailed from New Hampshire.

founder of the Republican party. As a United States senator from Ohio, he was a strong opponent of slavery. He served in President Abraham Lincoln's cabinet as secretary of the treasury, and later became chief justice of the United States Supreme Court.

ANOTHER PRESIDENTIAL CAMPAIGN

In recent years, it has become standard practice for presidential candidates to do some of their earliest campaigning in New Hampshire. In 1860, a congressman from Illinois, Abraham Lincoln, passed through the New Hampshire towns of Concord, Manchester, Dover, and Exeter, giving a series of political speeches. His listeners liked him, and the welcome they gave him helped him decide to run for the Republican presidential nomination. In the general election, he carried New Hampshire by a wide margin.

In 1861, soon after Lincoln became president, war broke out between the North and South. No Civil War battles were fought on New Hampshire soil, but New Hampshirites were staunch defenders of the Union. Some thirty-nine thousand men—nearly half of the state's male population—fought for the Union.

The 1860s were the only decade in New Hampshire's history in which the state's population decreased. The war took the lives of some thirty-four hundred men, and thousands of others left the state, following the advice of the New Hampshire native and prominent newspaperman Horace Greeley, who popularized the phrase "Go West, young man."

THE NORTH COUNTRY

At the end of the Civil War, the northern third of New Hampshire was still largely an unpopulated wilderness. In 1867, the state sold off 172,000 acres (69,607 hectares) of woodland in the White Mountains to private investors and speculators. The new landowners were anxious to reap the riches of the timberlands that had, up until then, been almost impossible to reach. One lumber tycoon, J. E. Henry, is reported to have said, "I never seen the tree yit that didn't mean a damned sight more to me goin' under the saw than it did standin' on a mountain."

The railroad interests were happy to cooperate in opening up the wilderness, and, in the 1870s, the rush to strip the mountains of their trees was on. Lumber companies would settle for a year or so in one location, working until the supply of wood was exhausted, then move on to another part of the forest. Left behind were hillsides covered with debris that invited disastrous forest fires; and streams, once clean and pure, now polluted and choked with tons of sawdust.

The opening of such luxurious resorts as the Mount Washington Hotel brought tourism to the White Mountains in the late 1800s.

State tax laws actually encouraged clear-cutting—stripping an area of all its trees. The damage done to the environment was not recognized by most people until the twentieth century.

The northern forests consisted primarily of spruce and fir trees, too small to be used profitably for cutting board. This wood was ideal, however, for the manufacture of pulpwood and paper. New Hampshire's hardwood forests supplied the materials for a variety of useful objects. Small woodworking factories sprang up; local manufacturers turned out bobbins, boxes, clothespins, gun handles, drying racks, bowling pins, crutches, bedsteads, and dozens of other wooden objects.

The trains that carried lumber out of the White Mountains brought a new source of income into the region—tourists. Dozens of large hotels were built—fancy places designed to attract wealthy customers. Several of them could accommodate four hundred or more guests. Railroad stations were built close to the resorts, and the rich and famous came off the trains in droves to enjoy the pure mountain air and spectacular mountain scenery.

Chapter 6

THE TWENTIETH CENTURY

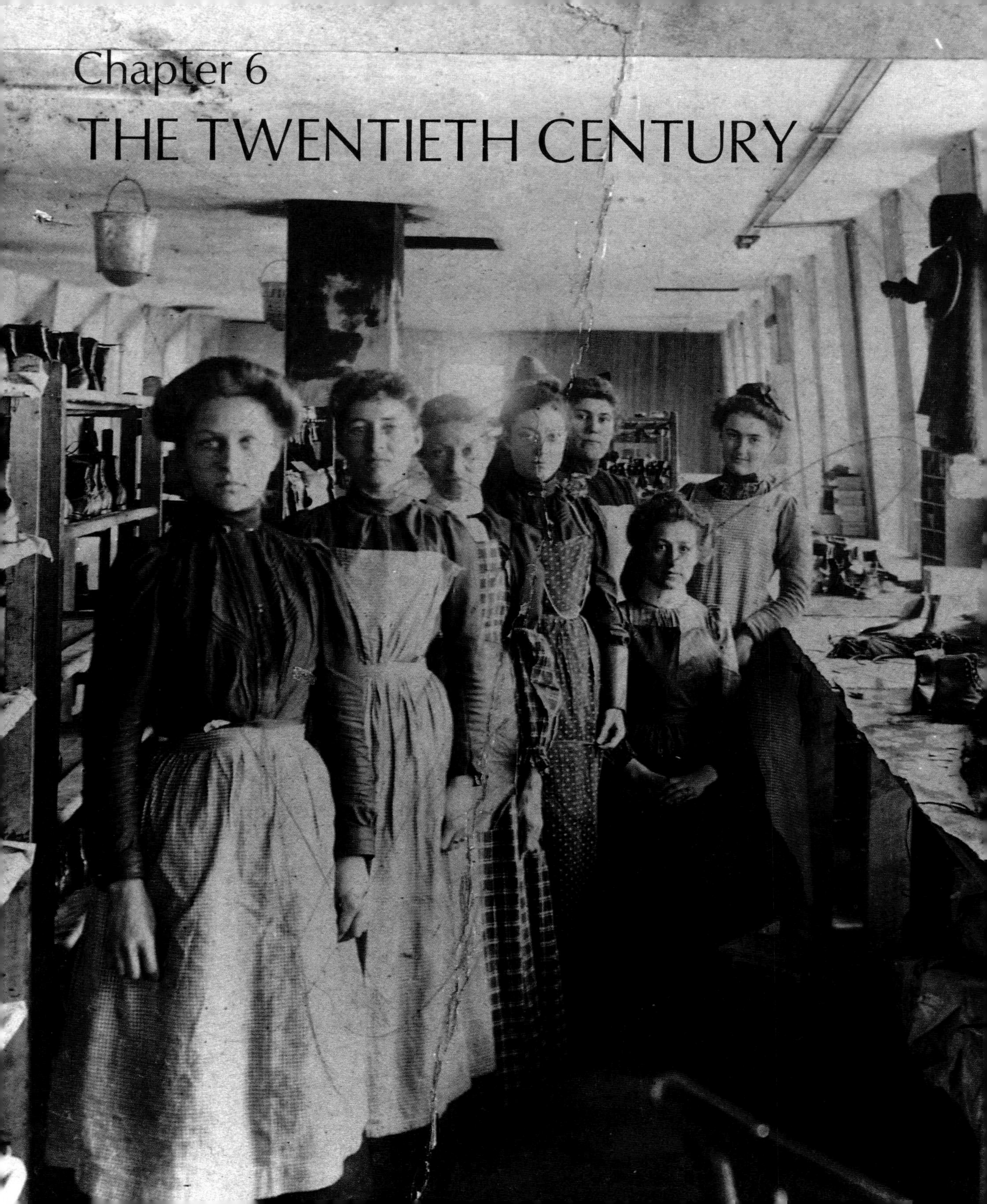

THE TWENTIETH CENTURY

As the new century began, more people in New Hampshire were making their livings from manufacturing than from agriculture. The railroads were still an important political power, and the lumber industry was still thriving. But several winds of change were beginning to blow.

Labor unions began forming in the shoe- and textile-manufacturing industries. A labor reform bill passed in 1907 limited the workweek for women and children to fifty-eight hours. Further bills passed a few years later called for factory inspections, regulation of child-labor laws, and compensation for workers injured on the job.

The Society for the Protection of New Hampshire Forests was founded for the purpose of regaining and saving those forests in the White Mountains that had been sold to private interests. Raging forest fires destroyed 12,000 acres (4,856 hectares) in northern New Hampshire in 1903. A 1911 law authorized the federal government to establish a national forest on 722,000 acres (292,186 hectares) of land in the White Mountains.

A state highway department was created to improve the roads, where a few automobiles were beginning to appear. Soon the railroad companies began to complain about competition from trucks carrying freight—an endeavor that up until then had been the monopoly of the railroads.

WORLD WAR I

When the United States entered the war in Europe in 1917, New Hampshire sent more than 20,000 men into service. By war's end, 697 New Hampshirites had lost their lives. The Portsmouth Naval Shipyard built warships, including submarines, for the United States Navy. Within a few years, submarine construction and repair became the main activity at the shipyard.

POSTWAR BOOM AND BUST

Manufacturers reaped high profits during the war, but a postwar slump followed. In Berlin, the International Paper Company cut wages by 30 percent, and workers responded with a strike. Lasting for several months, it was finally broken by the company.

The 1920s brought the demise of New England textile milling. Not even the Amoskeag Manufacturing Company, which by the early 1920s had become one of the largest cotton and woolen textile mills in the world, was immune. The company began to feel the competition of mills in the South, where wages were even lower than in New Hampshire. The machinery was getting old, and company management was reluctant to plow profits back into modernization. The advent of the fabric rayon caused a drop in the demand for cotton, and business slowed. Wages were cut in 1920 and again in 1921, and workloads were increased. In response, the workers went on strike. Labor disputes resulted in strikes at other New England textile mills as well.

In October 1929, the entire nation felt the shock of the New York stock market crash. Layoffs in factory after factory meant economic disaster for thousands of people. In 1936, after fifteen

Nashua was among the towns damaged by the devastating flood of 1936.

years of decline, the Amoskeag company shut down altogether. The company's investors declared bankruptcy, and withdrew their money, leaving eleven thousand people in Manchester out of work.

Natural disasters in the 1930s caused further hardships for New Hampshire residents. A devastating flood in 1936 caused more than $8 million in property damage. Two years later, a monster hurricane destroyed more than $50 million worth of property.

Yankee ingenuity and courage saved Manchester from becoming a ghost town. A group of citizens formed a company called Amoskeag Industries. They acquired the old Amoskeag mill properties, planning to lease out space to a variety of small companies. Within a few years, more than a hundred businesses were housed in the complex once occupied by the giant textile company.

Submarines were produced in Portsmouth during World War II.

WORLD WAR II

Democrat Franklin D. Roosevelt was elected president of the United States in 1932, 1936, 1940, and 1944. He received only 49 percent of New Hampshire's popular vote in each of the first two elections, but carried the state with 53 percent in 1940. That year, President Roosevelt appointed Frank Knox, publisher of Manchester's *Union Leader*, as United States secretary of the navy.

Secretary Knox was soon faced with the huge job of rebuilding the nation's naval strength. An attack on Pearl Harbor, Hawaii, on December 7, 1941, destroyed about half the capacity of the United States Navy and plunged the country into World War II.

Production rapidly went into high gear at the Portsmouth Naval Shipyard. The yard produced a vast number of submarines; at one point during the war, it turned out two a week. This was in addition to other vessels—landing craft, torpedo chasers, and floating cranes. About twenty thousand people, many of them women, went to work at the yard.

Some sixty thousand New Hampshire men and women joined

U.S. Secretary of the Navy Frank Knox delivering a speech in 1941

the armed forces during the war, and thousands more worked in factories that had been converted to defense production. The agricultural sector of the economy boomed.

A FIERY NEWSPAPERMAN

When Frank Knox died, about a year after the end of World War II, his widow sold the *Union Leader* to William Loeb, a man who was to become one of the loudest voices of conservatism in the nation. His editorials condemned, without restraint, anything and anyone he considered to be left-wing. Not content with espousing his favorite causes in editorials, he made sure that the paper's news columns, too, were slanted in favor of conservatism.

Loeb believed in low taxes and economy in government. He stridently opposed all "broad-based taxes"—general sales taxes

Presidential candidate George Bush campaigning in New Hampshire on the day of the 1988 New Hampshire primary

and state income taxes. He was also opposed to tax-supported public works and welfare. Loeb exerted a strong influence on politics in New Hampshire for thirty-five years, until his death in 1981. Today run by Loeb's wife, the paper continues to follow a conservative line.

THE PRIMARY STATE

New Hampshire's official nickname is the Granite State, but in recent years, it has also become known as the Primary State. In 1913, the New Hampshire state legislature passed a law making the second Tuesday in March—the traditional date for most of the state's town meetings—the day on which party primary elections would be held. This was to save the voters from having to drive their buggies into town an extra time. It was only coincidental that, as a consequence, each presidential election year, New Hampshire would be the first state in the nation to hold its primary.

In the years since World War II, presidential primaries have become important testing grounds for hopeful candidates. Every four years, nearly every announced candidate comes to New Hampshire to see how many votes can be gathered in this first of all state primaries. The results of the New Hampshire primary often determine whether or not a candidate continues to stay in the race.

Other states have tried to usurp the early attention New Hampshire receives by advancing their primary dates, but New Hampshire legislators refuse to let go of the lead. Current legislation guarantees that New Hampshire's primary will be held on the Tuesday preceding the primary of any other state.

Since 1952, no president has been elected without first winning the New Hampshire primary.

ENVIRONMENTAL CONFLICTS

The power of town meetings and home rule was tested in 1973 and 1974, when wealthy Greek businessman Aristotle Onassis tried to buy 3,000 acres (1,214 hectares) of land on Durham Point, near some of the earliest colonial settlements. He intended to establish a huge oil refinery and oil-tanker port in New Hampshire.

Concerned about a long list of environmental problems this development might cause, a citizens' group started a protest movement. Onassis and his supporters waged a huge public-relations campaign to convince people that the refinery would create jobs and not harm the environment. The people of Durham

Despite demonstrations against its opening, the Seabrook Power Plant began operation in July 1990.

took up the matter at their next town meeting. The vote against the project was nearly nine to one, and the state legislature upheld the rejection, deciding in favor of home rule.

In another controversy, New Hampshire environmentalists lost a lengthy battle. For seventeen years, from 1973 to 1990, a series of demonstrations, appeals, and court actions were waged over the construction of a nuclear-power plant at the coastal town of Seabrook. A group called the Clamshell Alliance led the struggle; they were joined by the Audubon Society of New Hampshire and various antipollution groups.

Opponents of the project managed to delay construction for many years. In 1986, public-opinion polls showed that 65 percent of New Hampshire voters opposed the project. Meanwhile, construction costs escalated to about $9 billion, driving the principal owner, Public Service Company of New Hampshire, into bankruptcy.

Nevertheless, Seabrook Station began operation in July of 1990, with one reactor on line. Plans to complete a second reactor have been abandoned.

Alan Shepard and
Christa McAuliffe

NEW HAMPSHIRE IN SPACE

On May 5, 1961, New Hampshire native Alan B. Shepard, Jr., earned a permanent place in history by becoming the first American astronaut to ride a rocket into space. Shepard's solo flight made him a national hero overnight.

Twenty-five years later, the entire nation mourned when Christa McAuliffe, a high-school teacher from Concord, was killed, along with six other crew members, in the explosion of the space shuttle *Challenger*. The National Aeronautics and Space Administration had chosen McAuliffe from more than eleven thousand applicants to be the first private citizen to ride into space. Just as millions of people had experienced awe and pride as they watched television images of Shepard's space entry, countless viewers cried on January 28, 1986, as they watched the *Challenger* explode just seventy-four seconds after lift-off.

In 1990, the people of Concord celebrated the opening of a new planetarium dedicated to the memory of Christa McAuliffe.

Chapter 7
GOVERNMENT AND THE ECONOMY

DANIEL WEBSTER

GOVERNMENT AND THE ECONOMY

New Hampshire is governed under the constitution of 1784. Every ten years, voters are given the option of calling a new constitutional convention. Any amendments proposed by such conventions must be accepted first by three-fifths of the state legislature, then voted on in a general referendum. Ratification requires a two-thirds majority of the voters. While it has been amended many times over the two hundred-plus years since it was written, the 1784 constitution remains the basic law of the state of New Hampshire.

STRUCTURE OF THE STATE GOVERNMENT

Like other states, New Hampshire has three branches of government: legislative, executive, and judicial.

Home rule—in which such small political units as towns or counties are allowed a large degree of self-government—has long been a guiding force in New Hampshire politics. Consequently, the first state constitution created a huge legislature and a comparatively weak executive branch. The legislature was set up so that representation is based on population, and the total number of members has fluctuated over the years. Today, New Hampshire's legislative branch, officially called the general court, is one of the largest legislative bodies in the world. It consists of two chambers: a twenty-four-member senate and a four-hundred-member house of representatives.

Every spring, each New Hampshire town holds a town meeting.

New Hampshire's executive branch of state government is unusual in that a five-person executive council shares some of the executive powers usually given solely to a state's governor. Both the governor and the members of the executive council are elected by a statewide vote to a two-year term. The governor, with the approval of the council, appoints the adjutant general, attorney general, commissioner of agriculture, and comptroller. The legislature elects the secretaries of state and treasury. There is no lieutenant governor. If the governor cannot serve, the president of the senate acts as governor.

Each branch of the legislature has the power to veto bills passed by the other branch, and the governor has veto power over acts passed by both branches. A two-thirds vote of members present in both bodies of the legislature is necessary in order to override a governor's veto.

The judicial branch includes a supreme court and superior court. All state and local judges, who may serve until they reach seventy years of age, are appointed by the governor with the approval of the executive council. The supreme court has a chief justice and four associate justices. The superior court has one judgeship for every sixty thousand residents of the state.

LOCAL GOVERNMENT

New Hampshire is divided, politically, into 221 towns, 13 cities, and 10 counties. The political and geographic unit called a *town* in New England is usually called a *township* in other parts of the country. The traditional New England town meeting—in which a town's voters meet for a day and vote on issues of local government—is the purest form of democracy in use today. Every spring, each New Hampshire town holds a town meeting. All the town's voters are given an equal chance to be heard. They then vote directly on the issues, rather than delegating that responsibility to an elected body of legislators.

In between town meetings, local government is run by three town "selectmen." Elected during the town meeting, they serve three-year terms, and one comes up for election each year. Also chosen at the town meeting are such local officials as the fire chief, town clerk, and treasurer.

TAXES

Taxes have always been a favorite topic of discussion in New Hampshire. Even before newspaperman William Loeb voiced his violent opposition to broad-based taxes, it did not take much to convince most New Hampshire voters that low taxes are to be preferred over higher ones. Historically, New Hampshire has been the most conservative state in the nation on the subject of taxes.

In 1939, the state legislature passed a tobacco tax to replace the annual direct tax on cities and towns. Liquor and pari-mutuel betting are also taxed. In 1963, New Hampshire became the first state in the twentieth century to hold a sweepstakes lottery for the purpose of raising public revenue. It proved so popular that other states soon followed suit. For many years, a major source of tax revenues from businesses had been the "stock-in-trade" tax. This was levied against any inventories held by companies past a certain date. The tax was not only unfair, it was also unworkable, since many businesses simply moved their stock out of state for a brief period when assessments were being figured. In 1970, the general court replaced this tax with a fairer one calculated on business profits.

Another tax was enacted that year on income—not that of residents but on income earned in New Hampshire by residents of other states. This tax was declared unconstitutional in 1975.

An attempt made in 1971 to levy a 3 percent income tax was not successful. New Hampshire still has neither a state sales tax nor a state income tax. Most of the educational needs of New Hampshire's towns are supported by property taxes, which, though lower than in many other states, are the highest in New England.

EDUCATION

Commitment to public education was written into New Hampshire's state constitution of 1784. Today, New Hampshire has about 450 public schools, and about three of every four adult residents of the state have graduated from high school. About

Left: Proctor Academy, a private
school in Andover
Above: Dartmouth students during
the college's winter carnival

18 percent of the state's residents have attended four or more years
of college.

Private academies were established in many New England
towns in the eighteenth and nineteenth centuries. Most
emphasized preparation for college, and for that reason became
known as "prep schools." New Hampshire's first such academy
was Phillips Exeter Academy in Exeter, founded as a boys' school
in 1781. Now coeducational, it remains one of the most famous
prep schools in the nation. St. Paul's School, in Concord, is

Dartmouth College, founded in 1769, is the nation's ninth-oldest college.

another distinguished private school. In all, New Hampshire has about twenty nonparochial private secondary schools.

New Hampshire has eleven private colleges. The oldest and best known is Dartmouth College, the ninth-oldest college in the United States. Founded in Hanover as a men's college in 1769, it became coeducational in 1972. Among New Hampshire's other fine private colleges are Franklin Pierce College, in Rindge; New England College, in Henniker; New Hampshire College, Notre Dame College, and St. Anselm College, all in Manchester; and Colby-Sawyer College, in New London. The leading public institution for higher education in the state is the University System of New Hampshire. It has four campuses: at Durham, Keene, Plymouth, and Manchester. The university system also offers the School for Lifelong Learning, founded in 1972 to provide credit and noncredit courses to adults in various communities throughout the state.

Tugboats in Portsmouth Harbor

New Hampshire has six private junior colleges, seven two-year vocational colleges, and two institutions offering graduate degrees only.

TRANSPORTATION

New Hampshire's 16,000 miles (25,749 kilometers) of highways and roads are not only well maintained and designed for safety, they are some of the most scenic routes in the United States. Trucks and railroads carry freight to many parts of the state. Five cities have public transit systems. The state's main airport is in Manchester. About fifty small airports and heliports are found throughout the state.

Portsmouth is an important international port, as it has been since New Hampshire's colonial days. Portsmouth's deep-water harbor is ice-free all year. More than 250,000 tons (226,796 metric tons) of cargo are shipped through the port annually.

A logging operation in northern New Hampshire

COMMUNICATION

Eight daily newspapers are published in New Hampshire, along with about forty other periodicals. The only morning daily, Manchester's *Union Leader,* is distributed statewide, with a circulation of approximately sixty-eight thousand. Other widely read New Hampshire papers include *Foster's Daily Democrat,* of Dover; the *Portsmouth Herald;* and the *Nashua Telegraph.* The *Boston Globe* has a significant New Hampshire readership.

Several magazines published in the state have a national circulation. Most noted are the *Old Farmer's Almanac* and *Yankee Magazine.* Several magazines devoted to information for computer users are based in New Hampshire. *Cobblestones,* a magazine for children, is published in Peterborough.

New Hampshire's broadcast industry includes about fifty radio stations, three commercial television stations, and three public television stations.

Commercial fishermen sorting out a catch in Portsmouth

AGRICULTURE AND NATURAL RESOURCES

Farming has been decreasing in importance in New Hampshire since World War II. Less than 8 percent of the state's land is used as farmland, and less than 1 percent of the state's total personal income is earned from farming.

Most of New Hampshire's farms are family-owned and operated. Leading farm products include milk, apples, eggs, corn, hay, poultry, beef, and hogs.

New Hampshire ranks second among the states in the extent of its forest cover. The Forest Resources Planning Act of 1981 regulates the use of New Hampshire's forests. The legislation's objectives are to improve the quality and mix of trees grown, maintain a core of wilderness areas, conduct wise wildlife management, and improve and maintain the water supply.

More than two hundred sawmills and several thousand logging operations employ about twelve thousand people in New Hampshire. New Hampshire trees are used to make paper, pulp, lumber and wood products, furniture, and wood fixtures. Young evergreens are sold as Christmas trees.

New Hampshire's ocean waters continue to provide good catches, especially of cod and lobster. The total value of New Hampshire's commercial fishing industry is more than $8 million a year.

Though the state is nicknamed the Granite State, mineral resources in New Hampshire contribute very little to the state's economy. New Hampshire's high-quality granite, however, is still quarried in the state.

MANUFACTURING

Manufacturing is New Hampshire's second-largest source of income. More people are employed in manufacturing than in any other type of work. Most of New Hampshire's companies are small, although more than thirty employers have a thousand or more workers. The state ranks very high among the states in the percentage of manufactured products that are exported.

In recent years, New Hampshire's major manufactured goods have been machinery, electric and electronic equipment, paper and pulp products, rubber and plastics, instruments and related products, leather, and such leather products as shoes. Textile manufacturing, once New Hampshire's most important industry, has slipped to seventh place on the list.

Cozy inns such as this contribute to New Hampshire's thriving tourist industry.

New Hampshire's economy grew at a faster rate than did the nation's as a whole during the 1970s and most of the 1980s. Much of this economic boom stemmed from the growth of high-tech industries. Southern New Hampshire and the nearby Boston metropolitan area became a world-class center for this new field.

SERVICE INDUSTRIES

Taken together, service industries—such as wholesale and retail trade, community and social services, finance, real estate, and tourism—constitute the largest source of income and employment in New Hampshire. The service industries associated with tourism—hotels, restaurants, entertainment facilities—are an important aspect of New Hampshire's economy. Each year, thousands of visitors come to the Granite State for summertime adventure, to view the spectacular autumn foliage, or to sample some of the best winter skiing in the East.

Chapter 8
ARTS AND RECREATION

ARTS AND RECREATION

New Hampshire has been an inspiration to artists for at least 150 years. In the nineteenth century, writer Nathaniel Hawthorne wrote stories set in the White Mountains, and John Greenleaf Whittier created poems about New Hampshire scenery. Henry Wadsworth Longfellow based some of his poetry on local legends. Early landscape artists found inspiration in the mountains. Maxfield Parrish, a noted illustrator of the early 1900s, painted pastoral scenes of the New Hampshire countryside.

Robert Frost, who spent most of his adult life in New Hampshire and Vermont, captured the soul of northern New England in his poetry. J. D. Salinger, author of the novel *The Catcher in the Rye*, lives a reclusive life in the southwestern part of the state.

New England was the nation's cultural center throughout most of the nineteenth century. Besides Whittier and Longfellow, poets Lucy Larcom and Celia Thaxter; essayists Ralph Waldo Emerson, Henry David Thoreau, and William Ellery Channing; and fiction writers Thomas Bailey Aldrich, Sarah Orne Jewett, and Kate Sanborn all traveled and vacationed in New Hampshire.

ART COLONIES

Sculptor Augustus Saint-Gaudens, whose statues stand in parks in New York City, Chicago, and Boston, fell in love with Cornish

New Hampshire's beauty has inspired many artists and writers, including Robert Frost, who lived in the state for many years (above); and Thomas Doughty, who painted this Echo Lake landscape (left) in the 1830s.

and made his home there in the 1880s. Soon, many of his artist and writer friends began spending summers at his retreat. They, too, became inspired by the surroundings. What became known as the Cornish Colony flourished for about fifty years, from 1885 to 1935. Paintings, poetry, drama, fiction, and architecture were among the artistic products of Cornish Colony members. Today, Saint-Gaudens's home, studio, and gardens are preserved as a national historic site.

Another art colony was formed in Peterborough, where composer Edward MacDowell spent his summers. After MacDowell's death in 1908, his widow and other supporters established the MacDowell Colony as a place where writers, composers, and visual artists could work in a quiet setting.

Above: An engraving depicting sculptor
Augustus Saint-Gaudens at work
Right: A bronze relief by Saint-Gaudens

Thornton Wilder wrote his masterpiece *Our Town* while living at the MacDowell Colony. Set in the imaginary town of Grover's Corners, New Hampshire, this classic play beautifully captures the flavor of a small New England town in the early 1900s.

Other artists who have spent time at the colony include novelists James Baldwin and Willa Cather, composers Aaron Copland and Leonard Bernstein, cartoonist Jules Feiffer, and poets Stephen Vincent Benét and Edward Arlington Robinson.

Still in existence, the colony today has more than forty buildings, including studios, residence halls, a library, and a social center. Four hundred acres (162 hectares) of woodlands surround the buildings. Talented artists are accepted as fellows and given lodging, meals, and studios in which to work.

The MacDowell Colony in Peterborough

THE STATE COUNCIL ON THE ARTS

The New Hampshire State Council on the Arts supports the arts in several different ways. The Arts in Education program provides funds for artists to spend a week or more in schools working directly with students and teachers. The New Hampshire Touring program helps local organizations bring performing-arts programs to schools, colleges, festivals, civic centers, and other institutions. The Rural Arts program supports performances, workshops, and lectures in small rural communities.

In addition, the council gives technical assistance and awards grants to individuals and organizations for the stimulation of artistic endeavors.

New Hampshire artisans continue to produce such traditional crafts as handwoven textiles (left) and Shaker-design boxes (right).

THE LEAGUE OF NEW HAMPSHIRE CRAFTSMEN

The League of New Hampshire Craftsmen Foundation was established in 1932 to encourage local arts and crafts. It underwrites statewide educational and exhibit programs and markets the work of local artists through shops in eight New Hampshire locations. The Craftsmen's Fair, held each summer since the 1930s, is the oldest annual crafts fair in the nation. The nine-day fair is held at Mount Sunapee State Park.

New Hampshire artisans continue crafts that were practiced here during the state's early days, such as the making of glass, furniture, and Shaker-design boxes. The League also publishes a Visual Arts Map, which lists about a hundred galleries, museums, and important historic sites in the state.

PERFORMING ARTS

The Peterborough Players, an Equity theater company, has been entertaining audiences each summer since 1933. Performances are held on a large farm near Peterborough.

The New Hampshire Music Festival's summer concert season includes performances at several locations in the Lakes Region. Concerts are also held in the parks during the summer season in Concord. The New Hampshire Symphony and New Hampshire Opera League present programs in the Palace Theatre in Manchester. Monadnock Music Concerts are given in several towns in southwestern New Hampshire during the summer. A popular summer-long arts festival held in Portsmouth's Prescott Park includes concerts, plays, classic films, and dance.

Programs cosponsored by the touring program of the New Hampshire State Council on the Arts include the work of a wide variety of performing artists. In the drama category, a recent schedule listed dance, folk dance, drama, storytelling, clown and magic acts, puppet theater, and mime. Musical concerts ranged from chamber music to jazz to pop.

Dartmouth College and the University of New Hampshire at Durham are cultural centers that draw audiences from all over northern New England to see high-quality theater, music, and dance performances.

RECREATION

New Hampshire has no cities large enough to support major professional sports teams, but the Boston Red Sox, Bruins, and Celtics, as well as the New England Patriots, draw plenty of fans from the Granite State.

Camping (above) and mountain biking (right)
are extremely popular in New Hampshire.

The Appalachian Mountain Club, organized in Boston in 1876,
constructs and maintains hiking trails and trailside shelters. Much
of its activity has been concentrated in the White Mountains of
New Hampshire. The New Hampshire Heritage Trail, now under
construction, will be a 230-mile (370-kilometer) route from
Massachusetts to Canada.

Fishing, hunting, camping, hiking, and mountain climbing are
popular outdoor sports. The state's numerous lakes and rivers are
playgrounds for swimming, boating, water skiing, kayaking, and
canoeing.

But it is winter sports that have really put New Hampshire on
the nation's recreational map. A snowshoe club was formed in

Left: Cross-country skiers near Bretton Woods
Above: A rock climber scaling Cathedral Ledge

Concord in 1887. The Dartmouth Outing Club, organized in 1909, soon inaugurated a winter carnival that rapidly became an annual event still popular today. Other towns in the state copied the idea, though few are as elaborate as Dartmouth's. The carnival features skiing, skating, hockey, and other winter sports, as well as an ice sculpture contest that always inspires spectacular work.

Skiing caught on in northern New Hampshire in the 1930s. Beginning in 1931, and for many years after, the Boston and Maine Railroad ran "snow trains" to transport skiers and other winter-lovers between Boston and North Conway. Today, there are dozens of ski trails, ski lodges, ski lifts, ski shops, and ski schools all through the White Mountains.

Chapter 9
A TOUR OF THE GRANITE STATE

A TOUR OF THE GRANITE STATE

Few spots in the world possess more natural beauty than the 9,279 square miles (24,033 square kilometers) of the Granite State. Mixed forests of evergreen and hardwood trees cover much of the land, a haven for wildlife and a paradise for campers and hikers. Add to that a sparkling Atlantic waterfront, hundreds of clear lakes and rippling rivers, and towering mountains etched against the sky.

The state's cities are clustered, for the most part, in the south. People in the rest of the state live in small towns or in the country. Villages have stately old homes and white-steepled churches on tree-lined streets. The buildings are often centered around a town square—usually called a "green" or a "common."

Our tour of the Granite State begins with the seacoast, where the earliest settlers from Europe entered the region.

THE SEACOAST

Strawbery Banke, the settlement that became Portsmouth, is New Hampshire's most significant visible legacy of colonial times. Ten acres (4 hectares) of the original settlement are preserved as an outdoor living-history museum. Here people can glimpse what life was like in earlier days as they wander through forty-two buildings dating from the 1600s to the 1900s. Many of the

The waterfront in Portsmouth

buildings have been completely restored, and archaeological excavations of the area are ongoing. Exhibits explain the processes of restoration, and guides interpret the history of the settlement. Artisans demonstrate such crafts as weaving, cabinetmaking, and boat building.

Several other mansions and historic homes in Portsmouth evoke Portsmouth's past glory as one of the world's great centers of international trade and shipbuilding. Sightseeing boats take passengers on cruises around Portsmouth Harbor, upriver, and out to the Isles of Shoals.

The Children's Museum of Portsmouth has hands-on exhibits on nature, computers, space, the arts, and geography, as well as a lobstering exhibit and a facsimile of a submarine.

East of Portsmouth, in the picturesque island town of New Castle, is Fort Constitution, site of the first act of overt resistance of the American Revolution. In 1774, several hundred New Hampshire patriots stormed the fort—at that time the British Fort William and Mary—locked up the British guard, and carried off

91

Phillips Exeter Academy is one of the nation's most prestigious prep schools.

military supplies and gunpowder. Nearby Odiorne State Park marks the spot where the first Europeans to settle in New Hampshire landed in 1623. A nature center at the park includes displays, slides, and films on sea life and marine topics.

Statues, fountains, fifteen hundred rose bushes, and a greenhouse with exotic plants make a visit to Fuller Gardens in North Hampton a delight. Hampton Beach, to the south, is a popular oceanside playground with a wide, sandy beach and a colorful boardwalk.

Two towns in the seacoast region are famous educational centers. Phillips Exeter Academy, founded in the town of Exeter in 1781, has been a prominent college preparatory school ever since. Three United States presidents—Abraham Lincoln, Ulysses S. Grant, and Grover Cleveland—sent their sons to Exeter. Durham, to the north, is the home of the main campus of the University of

New Hampshire. Its summer headquarters for the study of marine biology is located on the Isles of Shoals.

THE MERRIMACK VALLEY

The Merrimack River begins at the town of Franklin and flows southward into Massachusetts. As an early artery of transportation, and later as a source of waterpower for sawmills and gristmills, the river was responsible for the development of New Hampshire's major industrial centers.

Franklin was the birthplace of famed United States senator and orator Daniel Webster. The cabin he was born in is open to the public during summer months. Concord, south of Franklin, is a financial and manufacturing center as well as the seat of state government. Its best-known product in the nineteenth century was the Concord coach. An annual Coach and Carriage Parade Festival commemorates that part of the city's past.

The state house, in the center of Concord, is one of the nation's oldest state capitol buildings. It was completed in 1819 and has been remodeled and enlarged twice. Murals in the senate chambers, painted in 1942, depict scenes of New Hampshire history. Statues of some of New Hampshire's most famous sons stand on the state house lawn: Daniel Webster, Revolutionary War hero General John Stark, noted Civil War-era statesman John P. Hale, and Franklin Pierce, fourteenth president of the United States. Portraits of other noted New Hampshirites line the hallways of the capitol. Among them are astronaut Alan Shepard, Jr., and Mary Baker Eddy, founder of Christian Science.

The home that Franklin Pierce lived in from 1842 to 1848 has been reconstructed and moved to a site about a mile (1.6 kilometers) north of the state house. It is furnished with many

Original buildings (left) and traditional crafts (right) are on display at the Shaker Village at Canterbury.

original and period pieces and is open to the public during the summer. Pierce's childhood home in Hillsboro, about 20 miles (32 kilometers) west of Concord, is also open during the summer.

North of Concord is the Shaker Village at Canterbury, established in 1792. The Shaker religion, founded by Ann Lee in 1774, stressed community, religious discipline, pacifism, orderliness, simplicity, and productive labor. By 1845, eighteen self-sufficient Shaker communities had been established from Maine to Kentucky, and membership totaled four thousand. Today, fewer than a dozen Shakers remain.

More than twenty of the Canterbury settlement's original buildings have been preserved. Famous for their exquisitely crafted furniture, the Shakers have always been extremely industrious and inventive. The clothespin, circular saw, flat broom, and numerous other practical tools were originated by Shakers. They also pioneered the practice of gathering and

The Robert Frost Farm in Derry

packaging seeds for sale. Guided tours of the lovely pastoral
village give visitors a wonderful glimpse into the faith and
accomplishments of these remarkable people.

Manchester is New Hampshire's largest city. About four-fifths
of the brick factory buildings in the enormous complex once
occupied by the Amoskeag Manufacturing Company still stand.
Tours of the Amoskeag mills are available. Two fine museums in
Manchester are the Currier Gallery of Art, one of America's finest
small museums; and the Manchester Historic Association.

Southeast of Manchester, off Interstate 93 in the town of Derry,
is the Robert Frost Farm, where the noted poet lived for eleven
years. Open to the public during the summer, the farm has been
restored and is furnished with many family pieces. Displays and
films feature Frost's work.

Farther south, in North Salem, is Mystery Hill, sometimes called
America's Stonehenge. No one knows who built this strange

collection of stone walls, passageways, chambers, and carvings. Some people believe that it was an early European colonial site.

THE CONNECTICUT VALLEY

Exploring the villages of the Connecticut Valley and nearby hillsides is like looking through an old photo album or collection of postcards. Many of these towns look as if nothing has changed in the past fifty or sixty years—except for the television antennas that now appear on rooftops.

Near the Massachusetts border and about halfway between the Connecticut River and Nashua is the town of Rindge. The Cathedral of the Pines, a nondenominational outdoor shrine and memorial to all Americans killed in wars, is located here. A Memorial Bell Tower honors American women who have given their lives for their country. The altar is made of stones sent by several presidents and from all fifty states.

In Jaffrey, an annual public-speaking contest is held in the town's 1773 Meeting House. The Amos Fortune Lectures, as the contest is called, awards prizes funded by money left to the district school by a former slave. Amos Fortune managed to save enough money to buy his own and his wife's freedom, as well as to leave behind this unusual legacy.

Peterborough is the site of the MacDowell Colony. Parts of the colony can be visited, but the privacy of the artists at work here is carefully protected. A few miles north of the colony is the home of the Peterborough Players, a summer theater company that has been performing here for nearly sixty years.

Keene is southwestern New Hampshire's largest city. Its tree-lined main street is one of the widest in the world. Along several side roads south of Keene are half a dozen photogenic old covered

Saint-Gaudens National Historic Site in Cornish

bridges. East of Keene, on the way to Dublin, is the Friendly Farm. Here visitors can touch and feed farm animals and observe the kind of farm life that has almost disappeared from New Hampshire.

Old Fort Number 4, near Charlestown, is an authentic reconstruction of a fortified village built here in 1744. Craft demonstrations and battle reenactments bring eighteenth-century history to life.

Lake Sunapee, a few miles east of Claremont, has been a popular resort area for more than 150 years. Several boats take passengers on cruises of the lake. Mount Sunapee State Park is a large recreation area with hiking trails and facilities for both summer and winter sports. A chairlift carries skiers in winter and sightseers in summer to the top of the mountain.

Sculptor Augustus Saint-Gaudens lived on a beautiful hill in Cornish. His home, studios, and gardens are preserved as the

Marlow, a picturesque town in southwestern New Hampshire

Saint-Gaudens National Historic Site. National Park Service
rangers tell visitors about the many famous statues and other
works created by Saint-Gaudens.

The campus of Dartmouth College is the heart of Hanover, a
pretty town with well-kept homes, shops, restaurants, and college
buildings. The college's Hood Museum of Art has fine collections
of Asian, European, American, Native American, and African art.
Outstanding murals painted by José Clemente Orozco decorate the
walls of Baker Memorial Library.

A trip up the Connecticut River from Hanover takes one
through one lovely village after another—Lyme, Orford,
Haverhill—to name just a few. Orford has enjoyed the reputation
of being the fairest of them all ever since nineteenth-century
writer Washington Irving called it the most beautiful place he had
seen in all of the United States and Europe. A row of seven
mansions built between 1773 and 1839 by a leading architect of

Hikers on a ledge overlooking Squam Lake

the day overlooks the Connecticut River and the green hills on the other side of its banks.

CENTRAL NEW HAMPSHIRE LAKES

The map of central New Hampshire is filled with scores of lakes—some big, some so small they are called ponds. Summer homes, inns, and small resorts line the shores.

Lake Winnipesaukee is the largest lake of the region. Its shoreline is 283 miles (455 kilometers) long, and its many islands make it exceptionally scenic. Its name is a Native American word said to mean "Smile of the Great Spirit."

Millions of people have seen beautiful Squam Lake, northwest of Winnipesaukee, in a popular movie—though in the movie it had a different name. Katharine Hepburn, Henry Fonda, and Jane Fonda spent a summer here filming *On Golden Pond*. The Science

Lake Winnipesaukee is one of New Hampshire's most popular vacation spots.

Center of New Hampshire, on Squam Lake in Holderness, has 2 miles (3 kilometers) of nature trails and a collection of native wild animals displayed in realistic habitats. At the eastern end of the lake is the town of Center Sandwich. The Sandwich Historical Society Museums include an 1849 house, a country store and post office, a barn, and a transportation museum.

On the west side of Lake Winnipesaukee is Weirs Beach. Its attractions include a boardwalk, amusement park, marina, amphitheater, and a leisurely cruise around the lake on the Mount Washington Ferry. Its name comes from the fencelike fish traps, called *weirs*, that were once used by the region's Indians. In 1990, the state acquired a prehistoric site overlooking an ancient weir location along the Winnipesaukee River. This site will be used to educate the public about ancient North Americans.

A few miles south of Weirs Beach is Laconia, the main city of

The Conway Scenic
Railroad station
in North Conway

the Lakes Region. Three lakes lie partially within Laconia's city
limits. Gunstock, a year-round recreation area, is east of the city.
Farther west, on Newfound Lake, is the Audubon Society's
Paradise Point Nature Center, which offers a variety of nature
programs during the summer.

THE WHITE MOUNTAINS AND THE NORTH COUNTRY

The White Mountains are the heart of New Hampshire's
tourism industry. The first hotel in the White Mountains was built
in 1803. Much of the region is contained within the boundaries of
the White Mountain National Park. It is a natural wonderland of
sharp peaks, clear streams, deep "notches" (called "passes" or
"cuts" in other mountainous areas), lakes and ponds, and
wilderness. The Appalachian Trail, which winds through the
mountains from Maine to Georgia, provides hikers with
spectacular views. Eight hostels for hikers lie along New
Hampshire's section of the trail.

Moonrise over Mount Washington

State Route 16, on the eastern side of the Presidential Range, runs through Mount Washington Valley. The commercial center of the valley is North Conway. Its main street, lined with factory outlet stores and motels, is bumper-to-bumper and elbow-to-elbow with tourists for much of the year. A great view of Mount Washington—the highest peak in the Northeast—can be seen from the center of town. Every road out of North Conway leads through extraordinary scenery. The Conway Scenic Railroad tours the Saco River Valley several times each day in the summer. Canoeing and kayaking on the Saco are popular activities.

An antique car museum in Glen, north of North Conway, has a collection of automobiles manufactured over a fifty-year period. Storyland, a small theme park, features rides, entertainment, and exhibits appealing to young people. Next door is Heritage New

Hampshire, where life-size theatrical sets, state-of-the-art technology, and period characters bring to life three hundred years of New Hampshire history.

Tuckerman's Ravine, said to be one of the most challenging runs in this part of the world, is one of several ski areas near Pinkham Notch. A gondola tramway carries passengers from the notch to the top of Wildcat Mountain.

An auto road, open only from mid-May to mid-October, leads from nearby Glen House to the top of Mount Washington. There are three ways to scale this mountain—on foot, by auto on this road, and by cog railway from Crawford Notch.

A loop tour that covers most of the most popular spots in the White Mountains leads west and northwest from North Conway and Glen to Twin Mountain, west and then south to North Woodstock, and east on the Kancamagus Highway back to Conway. The Kancamagus Highway, named for an important Indian leader in the state, is one of New Hampshire's best-known attractions. It provides spectacular views as it takes travelers through uninhabited forestland along the Swift River.

The Attitash Alpine Slide at Bartlett has water slides, a chairlift, and a craft village. Three waterfalls tumble off the mountains near the highway in the vicinity of Crawford Notch.

The oldest man-made attraction in New Hampshire is the Mount Washington Cog Railway, completed in 1869. Steam-powered trains make several trips a day in summer to the top of Mount Washington and back. They chug slowly up unbelievably steep grades, with frequent pull-overs to sidings to let descending trains go by. The 3-mile (5-kilometer) ascent takes about an hour and fifteen minutes.

Poet Robert Frost once lived near Franconia. His home, now open to the public, is filled with memorabilia. Resident poets give

An aerial tramway takes skiers to the summit of Cannon Mountain.

readings in the old barn each summer. Nearby is Cannon
Mountain Aerial Tramway. The original aerial tram at this
location was the first in the nation. Beside the tramway is the
New England Ski Museum.

Many people consider Franconia Notch the most beautiful part
of the White Mountains. Several large hotels brought summer
visitors to Franconia Notch during the 1800s. Though the large
inns no longer exist, dozens of motels, country inns, and ski
lodges are close by. In summer and fall, the highways are filled
with sightseers who have come to see the natural attractions
associated with this notch. Echo Lake, The Basin, and Profile Lake
are all beautiful bodies of water. The Flume is an 800-foot
(244-meter) gorge between 70-foot (21-meter) sheer rock walls.
Buses carry visitors to within a quarter-mile (0.4 kilometers) of
the gorge, and boardwalks and walking trails continue on past
waterfalls and cliffs to a pool. Rare mountain flowers grow beside
the trails.

Beautiful Echo Lake is one of the attractions of Franconia Notch State Park.

Profile Lake is named for the rocky outcropping that overlooks it—the Old Man of the Mountain. The profile of the Old Man can be seen clearly from a viewing point beside the lake. This unusual natural monument has become a cherished symbol of the state of New Hampshire. The formation was first noticed by white settlers in 1805. Nathaniel Hawthorne wrote a story about it called "The Great Stone Face," and by the middle of the 1800s, it had become a popular tourist destination.

Clark's Trading Post, on the highway near North Woodstock, is one of the oldest commercial attractions in the White Mountains. It includes entertainment and rides on a steam train.

West of North Woodstock is Lost River, a stream that winds through glacial caverns and potholes, sometimes completely disappearing. At the foot of the gorge it becomes Paradise Falls. Trails and boardwalks lead through and over several caverns. Some three hundred native plants are displayed and labeled in Lost River Nature Garden.

Farther north, a few miles east of Lancaster, is Santa's Village, a small Christmas-theme park with animals, birds, rides, and entertainment. As one continues north, the villages become farther and farther apart, the woods deeper, the roads less traveled. The Androscoggin River courses along the east side of the state, past timberlands and the largest city of the North Country, Berlin (pronounced with the accent on the first syllable). Berlin is the home of the largest manufacturer of specialty papers in the United States.

The northernmost notch in the mountains is Dixville Notch, which has two claims to fame. The first is The Balsams, the last of the great White Mountain resorts. A tree-lined lake separates the highway from the imposing white stucco hotel. One by one, the rest of the resorts that catered to the rich and famous of earlier days have fallen on hard times and closed, but The Balsams still flourishes.

Dixville Notch is famous also because every four years, the first presidential election returns are announced from there. On the eve of election day, the few residents of the town gather at The Balsams in the evening. An individual voting booth has been built

Fall scenes in the White Mountain National Forest

for each registered voter. At the stroke of midnight, all of the voters enter their booths, mark their ballots, and place them in a box. The town's first selectman (the equivalent of a mayor) opens the box, counts the ballots by hand, and announces the results. Dozens of reporters are on hand to tell the world which candidate won in the first town in the nation to report its voting results.

From Portsmouth to Hanover, from Nashua to Dixville Notch, New Hampshire is blessed with magnificent scenery, abundant natural resources, and enterprising people. First state to write its own constitution, first to hold presidential primaries, it is appropriate that we leave it here in Dixville Notch, whose citizens take pleasure in casting the first votes in every presidential election.

FACTS AT A GLANCE

GENERAL INFORMATION

Statehood: June 21, 1788, ninth state

Origin of Name: In 1629, Captain John Mason named the colony of New Hampshire for his native county of Hampshire in England.

State Capital: Concord

State Nickname: Granite State

State Flag: The state seal, surrounded by a yellow wreath of laurel leaves interspersed with nine stars, is centered on a field of blue. The nine stars symbolize New Hampshire being the ninth state in the Union.

State Motto: "Live free or die"; words written by General John Stark on July 31, 1809, and adopted as the state motto in 1945

State Bird: Purple finch

State Flower: Purple lilac

State Tree: White birch

State Animal: White-tailed deer

State Amphibian: Red-spotted newt

State Insect: Ladybug

State Mineral: Beryl

State Gem: Smoky quartz

State Rock: Granite

A sleigh ride in Canterbury

State Song: "Old New Hampshire," words by John F. Holmes, music by Maurice Hoffman, Jr., adopted as the state song in 1949:

With a skill that knows no measure,
From the golden store of Fate
God, in His great love and wisdom,
Made the rugged Granite State;
Made the lakes, the fields, the forests;
Made the rivers and the rills;
Made the bubbling, crystal fountains
Of New Hampshire's Granite Hills.

Old New Hampshire, Old New Hampshire,
Old New Hampshire, grand and great,
We will sing of Old New Hampshire,
Of the dear old Granite State.

Builded He New Hampshire glorious
From the borders to the sea;
And with matchless charm and splendor
Blessed her for eternity.
Hers, the majesty of mountain;
Hers, the grandeur of the lake;
Hers, the truth as from the hillside
Whence her crystal waters break.

POPULATION

Population: 920,610, forty-second among the states (1980 census)

Population Density: 99 people per sq. mi. (38 per km²)

Population Distribution: In 1980, about 52 percent of the population lived in cities and towns, well below the U.S. average, and 48 percent lived in rural areas. More than half the people live in the state's thirteen incorporated cities. More than two-thirds of the state's residents live in southeastern New Hampshire.

Manchester 90,936
Nashua. 67,865
Concord. 30,400
Portsmouth 26,254
Salem 24,124
Dover 22,377
Keene 21,449
(Population figures according to 1980 census)

Population Growth: The estimated 1987 population figure for New Hampshire was 1,057,000, representing a growth rate of 14.8 since 1980, the highest in New England. The list below shows the state's population growth since 1790:

Year	Population
1790	141,885
1800	183,858
1820	244,161
1840	284,574
1860	326,073
1880	346,991
1900	411,588
1920	443,083
1930	465,293
1940	491,524
1950	533,242
1960	606,921
1970	737,681
1980	920,610

GEOGRAPHY

Borders: New Hampshire is bordered on the north by the Canadian province of Quebec, on the east by Maine and the Atlantic Ocean, on the south by Massachusetts, and on the west by Vermont and Quebec. New Hampshire also includes the three southernmost of the nine Isles of Shoals, which lie 9 mi. (14 km) off the Atlantic coast.

A covered bridge on the Swift River

Highest Point: Mount Washington, 6,288 ft. (1,917 m) above sea level

Lowest Point: Sea level, along the Atlantic Ocean

Greatest Distances: East to west—93 mi. (150 km)
North to south—180 mi. (290 km)

Area: 9,279 sq. mi. (24,033 km²)

Rank in Area Among the States: Forty-fourth

Rivers: New Hampshire's main rivers rise in the mountainous north. Among the principal rivers is the Connecticut, which begins near the Canadian border and forms the state's boundary with Vermont. The Merrimack, formed where the Pemigewasset River meets the Winnipesaukee River in Franklin, flows south and connects Concord, Manchester, and Nashua. The Salmon Falls and Piscataqua rivers form part of the border between New Hampshire and Maine. The Androscoggin River flows through the northeastern part of the state. Dams on the rivers provide waterpower for hydroelectric plants that supply electric power for public utilities. The dams form long lakes in the rivers.

Lakes: About two thousand lakes, ponds, and reservoirs are found throughout New Hampshire's hills and mountains. The largest is Lake Winnipesaukee, the sixth-largest natural lake located wholly within the U.S. It covers more than 70 sq. mi. (181 km²) and contains many islands. Other large lakes include First Connecticut, Francis, Newfound, Ossipee, Squam, Sunapee, Umbagog (which lies partly in Maine), and Winnisquam, and Moore Reservoir.

Topography: New Hampshire is generally hilly, rocky, and, in many areas, densely wooded. The state has three main topographical regions.

The Coastal Lowlands, in the extreme southeastern corner of the state, extend 15 to 20 mi. (24 to 32 km) inland from the Atlantic Ocean. The terrain consists of sandy beaches, salt marshes, and tidal inlets, as well as some meadowlands suitable for farming. The beaches of the coastline are popular recreational areas. The rivers of this area supply hydroelectric power for industry.

Most of the southern half of New Hampshire is part of a larger topographical region known as the Eastern New England Upland. In New Hampshire, this region includes the Merrimack Valley, the Hills and Lakes area, and the New Hampshire portion of the Connecticut River Valley. Crops of hay and fruits are grown in the rich soil of the Merrimack Valley, and New Hampshire's chief mill and factory towns are here. The Hills and Lakes area, surrounding the Merrimack Valley on the east, north, and west, contains most of the state's large lakes. The Connecticut River Valley, which stretches for 211 mi. (340 km) along New Hampshire's border with Vermont, has rich farmland in the lowlands and hardwood trees on the hills.

North of the uplands region, the White Mountains, part of the Appalachian chain, rise sharply from wide, flat areas that were lakes thousands of years ago. The area's forests provide wood for the state's paper mills. The White Mountains attract both summer and winter tourists.

Climate: New Hampshire has a changeable climate, with a wide variance in daily and seasonal temperatures. Summers are short and cool; winters are long and cold. The average temperature in July is about 66° F. (19° C) in the north and 70° F. (21° C) in the south. January temperatures average about 16° F. (-9° C) in northern New Hampshire and 20° F. (-7° C) in southern New Hampshire. The highest temperature ever recorded in the state was 106° F. (41° C), at Nashua on July 4, 1911. The record low temperature was -46° F. (-43° C), at Pittsburg on January 28, 1925. An average of 42 in. (107 cm) of precipitation falls on New Hampshire each year. The state's yearly snowfall can range from about 50 in. (127 cm) near the Atlantic Ocean to more than 150 in. (381 cm) in the mountains.

NATURE

Trees: Balsam firs, cedars, hemlocks, pines, spruces, tamaracks, ashes, basswoods, beeches, elms, maples, oaks, hickories

Wild Plants: American elders, gentians, chokeberries, red osiers, violets, black-eyed Susans, daisies, fireweed, goldenrod, purple trillium, wild asters

Animals: Opossums, squirrels, rabbits, moles, shrews, moose, bats, raccoons, chipmunks, mink, porcupines, muskrats, beavers, snowshoe hares, foxes, white-tailed deer, lynx, black bears, elk, martens, eastern coyotes

Birds: Ruffed grouse, pheasants, ducks, robins, chickadees, woodpeckers, blue jays, sparrows, purple finches, sparrows, warblers, artic terns, eastern bluebirds, ospreys, purple martins, whippoorwills

Fish: Trout, largemouth and smallmouth bass, landlocked salmon, pickerel, perch, whitefish, bullhead, cod, cunners, cusk, flounder, haddock, hake, mackerel, pollack, tuna

GOVERNMENT

New Hampshire's constitution was adopted in 1784. Under the constitution, New Hampshire has three branches of government—executive, judicial, and legislative. The governor, who must be at least thirty years of age, is elected by the state's voters to a two-year term. The governor is assisted by a five-member executive council, whose members are also elected to two-year terms. The council must approve all administrative and judicial appointments. The major executive officials appointed, with the approval of the council, include the adjutant general, attorney general, commissioner of agriculture, and the comptroller. The secretary of state and secretary of the treasury are elected by the legislature for two-year terms. New Hampshire has no lieutenant governor.

New Hampshire's legislature, called the general court, is one of the largest legislative bodies in the world. It consists of two chambers: a twenty-four member senate, and a four-hundred-member house of representatives. All state legislators are elected to two-year terms.

The judicial branch interprets the laws and tries cases. All judges in New Hampshire are appointed by the governor subject to confirmation by the executive council. Judges must retire at the age of seventy. The supreme court, the state's highest court, has a chief justice and four associate justices. The superior court, made up of fourteen associate justices and a chief justice, is the main trial court. In all categories, crime rates in New Hampshire are among the lowest in the nation.

In local government, New Hampshire continues to utilize one of the purest forms of democracy—the town meeting. Once a year, each of New Hampshire's 221 towns holds a meeting at which the voters choose selectmen (the chief local administrative officials) and other local officials, approve budgets, and decide local issues. Most towns have three selectmen. They serve three-year terms, and every year, one of the three comes up for election. Some of the larger towns have five selectmen.

New Hampshire's thirteen incorporated municipalities are governed either by a city manager or by a mayor and city council. The cities have home rule, meaning that they have large powers of self-government. New Hampshire has ten counties, each governed by three commissioners. Other elected county officials include the sheriff, attorney, treasurer, register of deeds, and register of probate. County officials are elected for two-year terms.

Number of Counties: 10

U.S. Representatives: 2

Electoral Votes: 4

Voting Qualifications: Eighteen years of age

This one-room schoolhouse in East Washington was built in 1849.

EDUCATION

New Hampshire's long-standing commitment to education dates back to colonial days, when students attended one-room schoolhouses. Some of those early schoolhouses still stand.

A seven-member state board of education and a commissioner of education govern the state's school supervisory unions. A supervisory union is an administrative grouping of the schools in neighboring towns or within a city. The governor and his executive council appoint the members of the board of education, and the board members elect the commissioner of education.

Children between the ages of six and sixteen must attend school. In 1980, more than 72 percent of all adult state residents were high school graduates; more than 18 percent had four or more years of college.

The best-known and oldest of New Hampshire's eleven private colleges is Dartmouth College, established in Hanover in 1769. Other fine private colleges include Franklin Pierce College, in Rindge; New England College, in Henniker; New Hampshire College, Notre Dame College, and St. Anselm College, all in Manchester; and Colby-Sawyer College, in New London. The University of New Hampshire, the state's leading public institution, originated at Hanover in 1866 and relocated to Durham in 1891. Today it is part of the University System of New Hampshire, which includes campuses at Plymouth, Keene, and Manchester.

ECONOMY AND INDUSTRY

Principal Products:
Agriculture: Milk, apples and other fruits, hay, potatoes, corn, poultry, eggs, beef, hogs, Christmas trees
Manufacturing: Machinery, electric and electronic equipment, paper and pulp products, leather goods, textiles and apparel, processed foods, rubber and plastic products, furniture
Mining: Granite, sand and gravel, mica, feldspar, beryl
Fishing: Lobsters, clams, crabs, cod, haddock

Business and Trade: Taken together, such service industries as wholesale and retail trade, community and social services, finance, real estate, and tourism make up the largest source of income and employment in New Hampshire. However, manufacturing is the largest single producer of income and employment in the state.

Communication: New Hampshire's first newspaper began publication in 1756 at Portsmouth. Called the *New Hampshire Gazette*, it is now the weekly supplement of the *Portsmouth Herald*. By 1984, the state had nine daily newspapers with a combined circulation of more than two hundred thousand, and three Sunday papers with more than one hundred thousand readers. The leading newspapers are Manchester's *Union Leader*, the *New Hampshire Sunday News*, the *Nashua Telegraph*, the *Concord Daily Monitor*, Dover's *Foster's Daily Democrat*, and the *Portsmouth Herald*. *L'Action* is a weekly French-language newspaper published in Manchester.

New Hampshire's first radio station, WLNH, was founded at Laconia in 1922. Today, 28 AM and 19 FM stations, including a Public Radio station in Concord, broadcast in New Hampshire. The state's first television station, WMUR-TV, began operations at Manchester in 1954. Today, New Hampshire has 5 commercial television stations and 33 cable systems. The state's residents also receive broadcasts from neighboring Massachusetts, Vermont, and Maine.

Transportation: New Hampshire's industrial growth in the 1800s encouraged expansion of the state's transportation system. The state's first railroad, which linked Nashua and Lowell, Massachusetts, began operation in 1838. In 1920, the state had more than 1,200 mi. (1,931 km) of railroad track, but by 1986, only 355 mi. (571 km) of track were still in use.

New Hampshire has more than 16,000 mi. (25,749 km) of roads. The state's major highway, Interstate 93, is a north-south route across the middle of the state. Other major highways are Interstate 89, which connects Concord with Barre, Vermont; the F. E. Everett Turnpike, which runs from Manchester to the Massachusetts border; the New Hampshire Turnpike (Interstate 95), which parallels the Atlantic coastline; and the Spaulding Turnpike, which connects Rochester with Portsmouth.

Covered bridges in New Hampshire are sometimes called "courting bridges" or "kissing bridges" because young people took advantage of the privacy of a covered bridge to steal a kiss. The covered-truss bridges and wooden-ark bridges found in New Hampshire are composed of a roadway, wooden sides, and a roof. The size is sufficient to accommodate a loaded hay wagon—the roof provided protection from a sudden shower and the sides helped control a skittish horse. There are fifty-four covered bridges in New Hampshire. They are numbered, and this numbering system is used on state tourist maps. The bridge that joins Cornish, New Hampshire, and Windsor, Vermont, is the longest covered bridge in the U.S. The nation's oldest covered bridge is the Warner-Dalton bridge near Warner Village, built about 1800. Most of the state's covered bridges were built in the 1800s.

New Hampshire's main airport is Grenier Field in Manchester. There are more than fifty airports and heliports in the state.

SOCIAL AND CULTURAL LIFE

Museums: The New Hampshire Historical Society Museum, in Concord, features displays about New Hampshire history. The Manchester Historic Association Museum is another fine historical museum. Exhibits of mounted animals from many parts of the world can be seen at the Morse Museum in Warren. Concord is the home of the Christa McAuliffe Planetarium.

The state's finest art collection is housed in Manchester's Currier Gallery of Art. The Manchester Institute of Arts and Sciences and the New Hampshire Art Association, also in Manchester, feature changing exhibits. Dartmouth College's Hood Museum of Art has a vast permanent collection. Other art galleries and museums include the Arts and Science Center in Nashua, the University Art Galleries at the University of New Hampshire in Durham, the Dartmouth College Museum and Galleries in Hanover, and the Lamont Gallery at Phillips Exeter Academy in Exeter. The work of nationally known craftspeople is displayed at the gallery of the League of New Hampshire Craftsmen in Concord.

Libraries: New Hampshire's first free, tax-supported, public library was founded in 1833 at Peterborough. Many historians believe that this library was the first of its kind in the United States. Today, nearly every town in New Hampshire has a library. The State Library Bookmobile Service is used by many small communities and rural areas. Leading academic and historical collections are housed at Dartmouth College's Baker Memorial Library in Hanover; the New Hampshire State Library and the New Hampshire Historical Society Library, both in Concord; and the Ezekiel W. Dimond Library of the University of New Hampshire in Durham. The New Hampshire State Archives in Concord houses official state documents and maps, as well as original town, legislative, and county historical records.

Performing Arts: The Palace Theatre in Manchester, home of the New Hampshire Performing Arts Center, was built in 1914 as a theater for vaudeville and stage plays. Renovated and restored in 1974, it today hosts performances of the New Hampshire Symphony and the New Hampshire Opera League. The Hopkins Center at Dartmouth College, in Hanover, features musical and other cultural events through the year. The Monadnock Music Concerts are held in several towns of the Monadnock region during the summer. In July and August, the New Hampshire Music Festival is held in several towns in the Lakes region, including Meredith, Gilford, and Plymouth. A popular summer-long arts festival held in

Portsmouth's Prescott Park includes concerts, plays, classic films, and dance performances.

Sports and Recreation: New Hampshire provides beaches, lakes, and rivers for all kinds of warm-weather water sports; mountains and snow for winter sports; and hundreds of miles of scenic trails for hiking. One of the newest trails is the New Hampshire Heritage Trail, a 230-mi. (370-km) trail, which, when completed, will travel the length of the state from Massachusetts to Canada. The first section, in Franconia Notch, was dedicated in the summer of 1989. Sailing enthusiasts can choose from hundreds of lakes. The annual Whaleback Yacht Race is held in August. Many major national and international skiing events have been held in New Hampshire. Snowmobile races, sled-dog races, and winter carnivals are also held throughout the state. The best-known winter carnival is the Dartmouth College Winter Carnival in Hanover. Dartmouth College, which belongs to the Ivy League; and the University of New Hampshire, part of the Yankee Conference, participate in various team and individual sports. Plymouth State College is a strong Division III contender in the sports of football, basketball, hockey, and skiing. Thoroughbred horseracing and greyhound dog racing are other popular spectator sports.

Historic Sites and Landmarks:

Belknap-Sulloway Mill, in Laconia, was constructed in 1823 and is the oldest unaltered brick textile mill in the U.S. Once a hosiery mill, it has been turned into a cultural center.

Fort Constitution, in New Castle, was the site of the first warlike act of the American Revolution. A museum traces the history of the fort.

Fort No. 4, in Charlestown, is a reproduction of a fortified village built by settlers in 1744, during the French and Indian Wars. During the summer, costumed staff demonstrate early eighteenth-century crafts.

Robert Frost Farm, south of Derry, was the home of the famous poet from 1900 to 1911.

Greenfield Town Meeting House, built in 1795, is the oldest original meeting house in New Hampshire.

Orford Street Historic District, in Orford, includes The Ridge, site of seven historic houses built between 1773 and 1839. The house of John H. Wheeler, completed in 1816, was designed by an associate of famed architect Charles Bulfinch.

Franklin Pierce Homestead Historic Site, near Hillsboro, was the boyhood home of the only U.S. president to hail from the Granite State. Designated a National Historic Landmark in 1961, the house has been restored to reflect the period of the early 1800s.

Restored colonial houses at Strawbery Banke

Pierce Manse, in Concord, is the home where Franklin Pierce and his family lived from 1842 to 1848. Restored to look as it did during that time, it contains many Pierce family furnishings and personal effects.

Saint-Gaudens National Historic Site, near Cornish, preserves the home, studio, and workshop of one of America's most famous sculptors.

Shaker Village, in Canterbury, is a settlement founded in 1792 by the communal religious sect known as the Shakers. The buildings, furniture, and crafts on display at the site illustrate the Shakers' high standards of craftsmanship and design.

Strawbery Banke, in Portsmouth, is a restored maritime village with historic buildings dating from the 1600s to the 1900s. The site offers tours, workshops, lectures, and demonstrations of colonial crafts.

Daniel Webster Birthplace, near Franklin, is a two-room cabin housing many mementos of the boy who became famous as an orator, statesman, and lawyer.

Wentworth-Coolidge Mansion, in Portsmouth, was the residence of Benning Wentworth, New Hampshire's first royal governor.

Other Interesting Places to Visit:

Annalee Doll Museum, in Meredith, houses more than a thousand flexible felt dolls, three hundred of which are on display at any one time.

Cathedral of the Pines, in Rindge, is an outdoor shrine where all may worship. It has two national war memorials: the Altar of the Nation, which recognizes all American war dead; and the Memorial Bell Tower, which specifically honors American women killed in wars.

Conway Scenic Railroad, in North Conway, provides an hour-long, 11-mi. (18-km) round trip through the countryside in big red coaches pulled by an old-fashioned locomotive. The railroad's quaint 1874 depot has been preserved as a museum.

Franconia Notch State Park, in the White Mountains, is New Hampshire's leading tourist attraction. Included in the 8,500-acre (3440-hectare) park are the Flume, an impressive, 800-ft. (244-m) long chasm that boasts a gorgeous waterfall; the famous granite rock formation known as the "Old Man of the Mountain"; and an eighty-passenger aerial tramway at Cannon Mountain that offers views of spectacular scenery.

Heritage New Hampshire, north of Glen, is a museum that provides an audio-visual journey through three centuries of New Hampshire history.

Lake Winnipesaukee, near Laconia, is a popular tourist spot that offers such recreational activities as boating, fishing, and swimming. It is the largest lake in the state and the sixth-largest natural lake lying wholly within the U.S.

Mount Washington Cog Railway, near Bretton Woods, provides a 3-mi. (4.8-km) climb via quaint steam engines up Mount Washington, the highest point in New Hampshire. The track grade to the summit is the second steepest in the world and was the first of its type.

Mount Washington Hotel, in Carroll, was built in 1902. It has been host to presidents, royalty, and celebrities. In 1944, the U.S. government chose the Mount Washington Hotel as the site for the famed Bretton Woods Monetary Conference, which provided the world with badly needed postwar currency stability.

Mystery Hill, near North Salem, is a puzzling collection of stone walls, passageways, chambers, and carvings. Some people believe that it was an early European colonial site.

Ruggles Mine, near Grafton, is the oldest mica, feldspar, beryl, and uranium mine in the U.S. It first opened in 1803. Mineral collecting is permitted.

State Capitol, in Concord, is constructed of New Hampshire granite. Completed in 1819, it is the nation's oldest state capitol in which the legislature meets in its original chambers. The building was enlarged in 1864 and 1909.

White Mountain National Forest, in northern New Hampshire, is the largest area of public land in New England. The boundaries of the forest extend across New Hampshire into Maine. It contains twenty campgrounds, fourteen picnic areas, 1,200 mi. (1,931 km) of hiking trails, and numerous ski, fishing, and boating areas.

The Mount Washington Cog Railway

IMPORTANT DATES

c. 8,000 B.C.—New Hampshire is occupied by its earliest-known inhabitants

c. A.D. 1600—At the time of the arrival of the first Europeans, New Hampshire is inhabited by the Western Abenaki, a group belonging to the eastern branch of the Algonquian language family

1603—English captain Martin Pring explores the mouth of the Piscataqua River near the present site of Portsmouth

1605—French explorer Samuel de Champlain sails along the New Hampshire coast and discovers the Isles of Shoals

1614—English Captain John Smith sails along the Atlantic Coast and gathers information about Piscataqua Bay and the Isles of Shoals, which he names "Smith's Islands"

1620—King James I of England sets up the Council of New England, which, under the leadership of Sir Ferdinando Gorges, is given jurisdiction over all the land from the Atlantic to the Pacific ocean between 40° and 48° north latitude

1622—John Mason, called "the founder of New Hampshire," and Gorges receive a grant for a large tract of land in present-day New Hampshire and Maine

1623—David Thomson and a small group of colonists found the first permanent white settlement in present-day New Hampshire, at Odiorne's Point in Little Harbor (now Rye); at about the same time, Edward Hilton settles Hilton's Point (now Dover)

1629 — John Mason names his grant of land between the Merrimack and Piscataqua rivers *New Hampshire* after his native county of Hampshire, England

1634 — The first church built in New Hampshire is established at Dover

1638 — Exeter is founded by John Wheelwright, a clergyman banished from the Massachusetts Bay Colony for religious reasons; Hampton is founded by a group of Massachusetts Bay colonists led by Reverend Stephen Bachiler

1641 — The four New Hampshire settlements place themselves under the jurisdiction of Massachusetts

1647 — An act is passed requiring towns of fifty households to maintain a school for teaching reading and writing; towns of more than one hundred households must maintain a grammar school

1653 — Strawbery Banke is renamed Portsmouth

1679-80 — New Hampshire becomes a royal colony of England separate from Massachusetts, with a president and council appointed by the king and an assembly chosen by the people

1685 — New Hampshire unites with other American colonies to form the Dominion of New England

1689-97 — New Hampshire communities seek safety from Indian attacks in stockaded garrisons during King William's War, the first of the French and Indian Wars

1689-1763 — French and Indian Wars are fought, off and on, in New Hampshire and the rest of New England; New Hampshirites Robert Rogers, leader of a group of soldiers called Rogers' Rangers, and John Stark win fame as colonial military leaders

1717 — John Wentworth is appointed royal lieutenant governor of New Hampshire

1734 — A religious revival, known as the Great Awakening, sweeps New Hampshire

1740 — The eastern and southern boundaries of New Hampshire are established by a royal commission, thus settling the boundary dispute between New Hampshire and Massachusetts

1741 — Benning Wentworth is appointed the first independent royal governor of the province of New Hampshire

1756 — New Hampshire's first newspaper, the *New Hampshire Gazette,* is established in Portsmouth

1764 — New Hampshire's western boundary is established at the western bank of the Connecticut River, thus settling a boundary dispute with New York

1769 — Dartmouth College opens at Hanover

1774 — Paul Revere rides to New Hampshire to warn the people of a British military buildup in Massachusetts; some four hundred New Hampshire colonists seize military supplies from a British fort at New Castle

1775 — The Revolutionary War breaks out in Massachusetts; hundreds of New Hampshire "minutemen" hurry to Boston to join the fight

1776 — New Hampshire adopts a temporary constitution on January 5, becoming the first of the original thirteen states to establish a government wholly independent from Great Britain; on July 4, New Hampshire's delegates join those of the other thirteen states in signing the national Declaration of Independence

1784 — New Hampshire adopts a permanent state constitution

1788 — New Hampshire becomes the ninth state — and the decisive vote — to ratify the U.S. Constitution

1804 — New Hampshire's first cotton textile mill is established at New Ipswich

1819 — A power loom is introduced at the Amoskeag Mills in Manchester

1833 — The nation's first free, public, tax-supported library is founded at Peterborough

1838 — The first railroad in the state begins operation

1846 — Manchester, New Hampshire's largest industrial center, becomes the state's first incorporated city

1847 — The New Hampshire legislature enacts a ten-hour-workday law for factory workers

1853 — Franklin Pierce of New Hampshire is inaugurated fourteenth president of the U.S.

1861-65 — During the Civil War, approximately thirty-nine thousand men from New Hampshire fight for the Union; the Fifth New Hampshire Regiment suffers more casualties than any other regiment in the Union army

1866 — New Hampshire College of Agriculture and Mechanic Arts (later to become the University of New Hampshire) is founded in Hanover

1871 — The state legislature passes a law making school attendance compulsory

1905 — The treaty ending the Russo-Japanese War is signed at Portsmouth

1909—New Hampshire adopts the direct primary law

1917-18—During World War I, New Hampshire supplies some twenty thousand men to the armed forces, the state contributes $80 million to the war effort, and Portsmouth Naval Shipyard becomes an important builder of warships

1922—WLNH, the state's first radio station, begins broadcasting from Laconia; labor strikes affect New Hampshire's textile industry

1923—New Hampshire College of Agriculture and Mechanic Arts is renamed University of New Hampshire by an act of the state legislature

1929—On the slopes of Sugar Hill, Austrian-born Sig Buchmayr establishes the first organized ski school in the U.S.

1930—The nationwide economic depression is felt in New Hampshire as some factories close and wages decrease

1936—Spring floods destroy more than $8 million worth of property; federal aid comes from Works Progress Administration (WPA) and Civilian Conservation Corps (CCC)

1941-45—During World War II, New Hampshire contributes men, women, and money to the war effort, and Portsmouth again becomes a major shipbuilding center

1944—The International Monetary Conference is held at Bretton Woods

1954—WMUR-TV, New Hampshire's first television station, begins telecasting from Manchester

1961—Alan B. Shepard, Jr., of New Hampshire becomes the first American to travel in space

1962—Thorium deposits, vital to nuclear fuel, are discovered in the White Mountains

1963—The New Hampshire sweepstakes lottery, the nation's first legal lottery since 1894, is approved

1966—Home rule is granted to New Hampshire cities; the Environmental Protection Agency approves New Hampshire's clean air plans

1973—Construction of an atomic energy plant at Seabrook is approved by the Atomic Safety and Licensing Board of the Nuclear Regulatory Commission; the agency rules that proper safety precautions are being taken

1977—Two thousand demonstrators march on the construction site of the nuclear plant at Seabrook; state police are called in to arrest those who refuse to leave

1978 — A February blizzard causes extensive damage throughout much of the state

1981 — On June 23, more than 80 percent of New Hampshire's state workers call in sick, as part of a protest for higher wages; gypsy moths cause severe defoliation in the state

1986 — Concord teacher Christa McAuliffe is one of seven crew members killed when the space shuttle *Challenger* explodes minutes after take-off

1988 — The Public Service Company of New Hampshire, a heavy investor in the Seabrook Nuclear Power Plant, files a bankruptcy plea

1990 — David Souter of New Hampshire is appointed associate justice of the U.S. Supreme Court; Seabrook Station begins operations

IMPORTANT PEOPLE

Sherman Llewellyn Adams (1899-1986), politician; U.S. representative from New Hampshire (1945-47); governor of New Hampshire (1949-53); chief of staff for President Dwight D. Eisenhower (1953-58)

Thomas Bailey Aldrich (1836-1907), born in Portsmouth; editor, author; editor of *Atlantic Monthly*; wrote novels, poetry, and stories, including the well-known "Story of a Bad Boy"

Josiah Bartlett (1729-1795), statesman, physician, American Revolutionary leader; New Hampshire delegate to the Second Continental Congress; signer of the Declaration of Independence; chief justice of New Hampshire (1788-90); governor of New Hampshire (1790-94); practiced medicine in Kingston for forty-five years

Amy Marcy Beach (1867-1944), born in Henniker; pianist, composer; performed with the Boston Symphony Orchestra; wrote *Gaelic Symphony* (1896), the first published symphonic work composed by an American woman

Jane Blalock (1945-   ), born in Portsmouth; professional golfer; winner of more than thirty professional tours

Elizabeth Gardner Bouguereau (1837-1922), born in Exeter; first woman to exhibit a painting at the Paris Salon of the French Academy of Art; first American woman awarded a gold medal by the Academy

THOMAS ALDRICH

AMY BEACH

LAURA BRIDGMAN

SALMON P. CHASE

STUART CHASE

BARBARA COCHRAN

Helen Dore Boylston (1895-1984), born in Portsmouth; author; used her experiences as a nurse to write the *Sue Barton* series of novels for children

Henry Styles Bridges (1898-1961), editor, teacher, politician; governor of New Hampshire (1935-37); U.S. senator (1937-61); known for his conservative views

Laura Dewey Bridgman (1829-1889), born in Hanover; first American blind and deaf person to be successfully educated

James Broderick (1927-1982), born in Charlestown; actor; appeared in many theater, movie, and television productions; best-known role was the father on the television series "Family"

Alice Brown (1856-1948), born in Hampton Falls; author of such children's books as *The Tiverton Tales* and *The Willoughbys*

Gladys Hasty Carroll (1904-   ), born in Rochester; author; wrote the regional novel *As the Earth Turns*, which was translated into sixty languages

Zachariah Chandler (1813-1879), born in Bedford; political activist; helped found the Republican party; U.S. secretary of the interior under President Ulysses S. Grant (1875-77)

Philander Chase (1775-1852), born in Cornish; clergyman, educator; Episcopal priest who founded Kenyon College in Ohio (1824)

Salmon Portland Chase (1808-1873), born in Cornish; statesman, lawyer, jurist; as a lawyer, gained fame for defending fugitive slaves; U.S. senator from Ohio (1849-55, 1860); governor of Ohio (1855-59); U.S. secretary of the treasury under President Abraham Lincoln (1861-64); laid the basis for the present national banking system; chief justice of the U.S. Supreme Court (1864-73); as chief justice, presided over the impeachment trial of President Andrew Johnson; his portrait is on the U.S. $10,000 bill

Stuart Chase (1888-1985), born in Somersworth; economist, author; advisor to President Franklin D. Roosevelt; coined the phrase "New Deal"

Jonas Chickering (1798-1853), born in Mason Village; piano maker; built the first grand piano with a full iron frame in a single casing (1837)

Nathan Clifford (1803-1881), born in Rumney; politician, jurist; U.S. representative from New Hampshire (1839-43); U.S. attorney general (1846-48); helped negotiate the Treaty of Guadalupe Hidalgo, which secured all or part of seven present western states, including California (1848); associate justice of the U.S. Supreme Court (1858-81)

Barbara Ann Cochran (1951-   ), born in Claremont; skier; won an Olympic gold medal in the women's slalom (1972)

Carroll Burleigh Colby (1904-1977), born in Claremont; author; artist; wrote nature and adventure stories for young people; wrote *Gobbit, the Magic Rabbit* (1951)

Ralph Adams Cram (1863-1942), born in Hampton Falls; architect, author; architect of the Cathedral of St. John the Divine (1911-12) in New York City

Mildred Custin (1906-   ), born in Manchester; business executive; first woman to head a major chain of retail stores; president of Bonwit Teller (1965-69)

Ralph Shepard Damon (1897-1956), born in Franklin; airline executive; helped produce a number of famous U.S. commercial and military aircraft, including the Curtiss Condor and the Republic Thunderbolt; developed the first "skysleeper" (1933); president of American Airlines (1945-49); president of Trans World Airlines (1949-56)

RALPH DAMON

Charles Anderson Dana (1819-1897), born in Hinsdale; editor, publisher; U.S. assistant secretary of war under President Abraham Lincoln (1863-65); owner and editor of the New York *Sun*, one of the most important newspapers of its time (1868-97)

Henry Dearborn (1751-1829), born in North Hampton; military officer; captain in the Revolutionary War; U.S. secretary of war under President Thomas Jefferson (1801-09); major general during the War of 1812; U.S. minister to Portugal (1822-24); Fort Dearborn at Chicago was named for him

HENRY DEARBORN

Edward Payson Dutton (1831-1923), born in Keene; publisher; founded the publishing house of E.P. Dutton & Company (1858)

Mary Baker Eddy (1821-1910), born in Bow; religious leader; founder of Christian Science, which teaches the healing of physical ailments through spiritual means; founded the newspaper *Christian Science Monitor* (1908)

MARY BAKER EDDY

Michael (Mike) Kendal Flanagan (1951-   ), born in Manchester; professional baseball player; pitcher for the Baltimore Orioles; won the American League Cy Young Award (1979)

Elizabeth Gurley Flynn (1890-1964), born in Concord; labor organizer; at age fifteen, helped organize the Industrial Workers of the World; president of the American Communist party (1961-64)

Daniel Chester French (1850-1931), born in Exeter; sculptor; created the seated statue of Abraham Lincoln for the Lincoln Memorial in Washington, D.C.; first important work was *The Minute Man*, completed when he was twenty-three

Robert Lee Frost (1874-1963), poet; spent much time in New Hampshire; wrote many poems about rural New England; won four Pulitzer prizes for poetry, including one for his collection *New Hampshire* (1924)

ELIZABETH FLYNN

SARAH HALE

JOHN IRVING

WILLIAM LOEB

Horace Greeley (1811-1872), born in Amherst; newspaper editor, political and social reformer; founder of the *New York Tribune* (1841); developed it into a widely read paper with a staff of distinguished writers; championed such causes as abolition, free common-school education, and agrarian reform

Sarah Josepha Hale (1788-1879), born in Newport; author, editor, educator; edited the magazine *Godey's Lady's Book* (1837-77); also wrote poems, including "Mary Had a Little Lamb," and a novel; founded the Seaman's Aid Society; was instrumental in ensuring the completion of the Bunker Hill Monument and in establishing Thanksgiving as a national holiday

Charles Francis Hall (1821-1871), born in Rochester; explorer, author; led various Arctic expeditions; wrote *Arctic Researches, and Life among the Esquimaux* (1864)

John Irving (1942-   ), born in Exeter; author; best known for his novel *The World According to Garp*; also wrote *The Hotel New Hampshire* and *The Cider House Rules*; many of his works have New Hampshire settings

Benjamin F. Keith (1846-1914), born in Hillsboro; theatrical manager, entertainer; in the 1800s, established vaudeville, a respectable, family type of entertainment; controlled some four hundred vaudeville theaters across the nation

John Langdon (1741-1819), born in Portsmouth; American Revolutionary leader; with his brother Woodbury, became a successful trader and shipbuilder; New Hampshire delegate to the Continental Congress and the Constitutional Convention; signer of the U.S. Constitution; governor of New Hampshire (1785-86, 1788-89, 1805-09, 1810-12); U.S. senator from New Hampshire (1789-1801); first president pro tempore of the U.S. Senate (1789)

William Loeb (1905-1981); journalist, publisher; influential publisher of Manchester's *Union Leader*; noted for front-page right-wing editorials; also publisher of the *New Hampshire Sunday News*

Stephen Harriman Long (1784-1864), born in Hopkinton; explorer, naturalist, army officer; as an army major, established Fort Smith, Arkansas (1817); led expeditions to the Upper Mississippi River (1817) and the Rocky Mountains (1820); Long's Peak in Colorado is named for him

Thaddeus S. C. Lowe (1823-1913), born near Jefferson; inventor, scientist, pioneer aeronaut; organized and directed a military balloon force during the Civil War; invented basic devices for atmospheric observation and metallurgical processing

Sharon Christa McAuliffe (1948-1986), born in Massachusetts; educator, community activist, astronaut; Concord high-school teacher who was chosen by NASA to be the first private citizen to ride into space; was killed, along with six other crew members, when the space shuttle *Challenger* exploded shortly after lift-off

John Mason (1586-1635), born in England; founded New Hampshire; named the colony after his native county of Hampshire in England

Grace de Repentigny Metalious (1924-1964), born in Manchester; author; wrote the best-selling novel *Peyton Place* (1956), which was adapted into a movie and a popular television series

Nicholas John Nicholas, Jr. (1939-   ), born in Portsmouth; president and chief operating officer of Time, Inc. (1986-   )

NICHOLAS NICHOLAS, JR.

Sarah Ellen Palmer (1856-1945), born in Exeter; physician; received an M.D. from Woman's Medical College of Pennsylvania (1880); became a Fellow of the American College of Surgeons when she was fifty-eight

Benjamin Pierce (1757-1839); military officer, politician; served in the Revolutionary War; governor of New Hampshire (1827-26, 1829-30)

Franklin Pierce (1804-1869), born in Hillsboro; fourteenth president of the U.S.; son of Benjamin Pierce; U.S. representative from New Hampshire (1833-37); U.S. senator (1837-42); served in the Mexican War (1846-48); president (1853-57); only U.S. chief executive to hail from New Hampshire

ALBERT READ

Charles Alfred Pillsbury (1842-1899), born in Warner; industrialist; turned a small flour mill in Minnesota into C. A. Pillsbury & Company, the largest flour producer in the world; using a new process for milling, the company produced ten thousand barrels of flour a day

Eleanor Porter (1868-1920), born in Littleton; author; wrote many popular short stories and novels, including the novels *Pollyanna* and *Pollyanna Grows Up*

Albert Cushing Read (1887-1967), born in Lyme; aviator; naval officer; commanded the Navy-Curtiss flying boat that made the first successful flight across the Atlantic (1919)

ROBERT ROGERS

Robert Rogers (1731-1795), military officer; grew up in New Hampshire; leader of Rogers' Rangers, a group of famous raiders who fought for the British army during the French and Indian War

Tom Rush (1941-   ), born in Portsmouth; blues singer, songwriter; albums include *Late Night Radio* (1985)

Augustus Saint-Gaudens (1848-1907), sculptor; lived for many years in Cornish, where he founded an artists' colony; his work, known for its lifelike quality, includes a statue of Abraham Lincoln in Chicago's Lincoln Park, a statue of Admiral David Farragut in New York City's Madison Square, and the *Shaw Memorial* in Boston

TOM RUSH

WILLIAM FRENCH SMITH

DAVID SOUTER

JOHN SUNUNU

CELIA THAXTER

Henry Wilson Savage (1859-1927), born in New Durham; theatrical producer; founded the Boston Light Opera Company (1895), which presented opera in English at a moderate price

Alan Bartlett Shepard, Jr. (1923-   ), born in East Derry; astronaut; making a solo flight in *Freedom 7*, he became the first American in space (1961); commanded *Apollo 14*, the third moon-landing mission

John Smith (1580-1631), English explorer; explored the Isles of Shoals (1614); explored and named New England; wrote a book, *A Description of New England*, that later guided the Pilgrims to Massachusetts

William French Smith (1917-   ), born in Wilton; U.S. attorney general under President Ronald Reagan (1981-84)

David Hackett Souter (1939-   ), jurist; moved to New Hampshire at age eleven; justice of the New Hampshire Supreme Court (1983-90) and the U.S. Court of Appeals, First District (1990); associate justice of the U.S. Supreme Court (1990-   )

John Stark (1728-1822), born in Londonderry; military officer; served with Rogers' Rangers during the French and Indian War (1754-63); had a distinguished record as an American general in the Revolutionary War; a statue of him represents New Hampshire in the U.S. Capitol in Washington, D.C.

Harlan Fiske Stone (1872-1946), born in Chesterfield; educator, lawyer, jurist; U.S. attorney general under President Calvin Coolidge (1924-25); associate justice of the U.S. Supreme Court (1925-41); chief justice of the U.S. Supreme Court (1941-46)

John Sullivan (1740-1795), born in Somersworth; Revolutionary War patriot, soldier, politician; led one of the first armed actions by colonists against the British, at New Castle; New Hampshire delegate to the the Continental Congress; governor of New Hampshire (1786-88, 1789-90); led the fight for New Hampshire's ratification of the U.S. Constitution

John Henry Sununu (1939-   ), engineer, industrialist, politician; governor of New Hampshire (1983-89); chief of staff for President George Bush (1989-   )

Celia Laighton Thaxter (1835-1894), born in Portsmouth; poet; works include the collection *Driftwood*

Earl Silas Tupper (1907-1983), born in Berlin; inventor, chemist; invented the plastic food and drink containers known as Tupperware; founded Tupperware Home Parties, Inc. (1945)

Meschech Weare (1713-1786), born in Hampton Falls; jurist, politician; justice of the superior court (1747-75); during the Revolutionary War, served as both chief justice of the superior court (1776-82) and first "president" (governor) of the state of New Hampshire (1776-85)

Daniel Webster (1782-1852), born in Salisbury (now Franklin); orator, lawyer, statesman; as a U.S. Representative from New Hampshire (1813-17), opposed trade restrictions and war; U.S. secretary of state under Presidents William Henry Harrison, John Tyler, and Millard Fillmore; first man elected to the United States Senate Hall of Fame

Benning Wentworth (1696-1770), born in Portsmouth; public official; royal governor of New Hampshire (1741-67); helped make New Hampshire independent of Massachusetts; Bennington, Vermont, is named for him

BENNING WENTWORTH

John Wentworth (1737-1820), public official; royal governor of New Hampshire (1767-75); fled New Hampshire at the outbreak of the Revolutionary War (1775); lieutenant governor of Nova Scotia, Canada (1792-1808)

Eleazar Wheelock (1711-1779), clergyman, educator; founder of Dartmouth College (1769); first president of Dartmouth (1770-79)

George Hoyt Whipple (1878-1976), born in Ashland; pathologist; shared the 1934 Nobel Prize for physiology or medicine for his research on the use of liver to treat animals with pernicious anemia

ELEAZAR WHEELOCK

William Whipple (1730-1785), American Revolutionary leader; New Hampshire delegate to the Continental Congress; signer of the Declaration of Independence; general in the Revolutionary War; associate justice of the state superior court (1782-85)

Henry Wilson (1812-1875), born Jeremiah Jones Colbath in Farmington; businessman, teacher, politician; ardent advocate of abolition; helped found the Free-Soil party; U.S. senator from Massachusetts (1855-73); helped found the Republican party; vice-president of the U.S. during the second term of President Ulysses S. Grant (1873-75)

WILLIAM WHIPPLE

Levi Woodbury (1789-1851), born in Francestown; politician, jurist; governor of New Hampshire (1823-24); U.S. senator (1825-31, 1841-45); U.S. secretary of the navy (1831-34); U.S. secretary of the treasury (1834-41); distinguished associate justice of the U.S. Supreme Court (1845-51)

Joseph Emerson Worcester (1784-1865), born in Bedford; lexicographer; his *Comprehensive Pronouncing and Explanatory Dictionary of the English Language* (1830) sparked charges of plagiarism from Noah Webster, resulting in the "War of the Dictionaries"

JOSEPH WORCESTER

Charles Augustus Young (1834-1908), born in Hanover; astronomer; in 1870, during a total eclipse of the sun, he observed the spectrum of the sun's corona, and proved the existence of the chromosphere; also determined the rate of rotation of the sun on its axis; wrote *The Sun* (1881)

GOVERNORS

Meshech Weare	1776-1785	Benjamin F. Prescott	1877-1879
John Langdon	1785-1786	Natt Head	1879-1881
John Sullivan	1786-1788	Charles H. Bell	1881-1883
John Langdon	1788-1789	Samuel W. Hale	1883-1885
John Pickering (acting)	1789	Moody Currier	1885-1887
John Sullivan	1789-1790	Charles H. Sawyer	1887-1889
Josiah Bartlett	1790-1794	David H. Goodell	1889-1891
John T. Gilman	1794-1805	Hiram A. Tuttle	1891-1893
John Langdon	1805-1809	John B. Smith	1893-1895
Jeremiah Smith	1809-1810	Charles A. Busiel	1895-1897
John Langdon	1810-1812	George A. Ramsdell	1897-1899
William Plumer	1812-1813	Frank W. Rollins	1899-1901
John T. Gilman	1813-1816	Chester B. Jordan	1901-1903
William Plumer	1816-1819	Nahum J. Batchelder	1903-1905
Samuel Bell	1819-1823	John McLane	1905-1907
Levi Woodbury	1823-1824	Charles M. Floyd	1907-1909
David Morrill	1824-1827	Henry B. Quinby	1909-1911
Benjamin Pierce	1827-1828	Robert P. Bass	1911-1913
John Bell	1828-1829	Samuel D. Felker	1913-1915
Benjamin Pierce	1829-1830	Rolland H. Spaulding	1915-1917
Matthew Harvey	1830-1831	Henry W. Keyes	1917-1919
Joseph M. Harper (acting)	1831	John H. Bartlett	1919-1921
Samuel Dinsmoor	1831-1834	Albert O. Brown	1921-1923
William Badger	1834-1836	Fred H. Brown	1923-1925
Isaac Hill	1836-1839	John G. Winant	1925-1927
John Page	1839-1842	Huntley N. Spaulding	1927-1929
Henry Hubbard	1842-1844	Charles W. Tobey	1929-1931
John H. Steele	1844-1846	John G. Winant	1931-1935
Anthony Colby	1846-1847	Styles Bridges	1935-1937
Jared W. Williams	1847-1849	Francis P. Murphy	1937-1941
Samuel Dinsmoor, Jr.	1849-1852	Robert O. Blood	1941-1945
Noah Martin	1852-1854	Charles M. Dale	1945-1949
Nathaniel B. Baker	1854-1855	Sherman Adams	1949-1953
Ralph Metcalf	1855-1857	Hugh Gregg	1953-1955
William Haile	1857-1859	Lane Dwinell	1955-1959
Ichabod Goodwin	1859-1861	Wesley Powell	1959-1963
Nathaniel S. Berry	1861-1863	John W. King	1963-1969
Joseph A. Gilmore	1863-1865	Walter R. Peterson, Jr.	1969-1973
Frederick Smyth	1865-1867	Meldrim Thomson, Jr.	1973-1979
Walter Harriman	1867-1869	Hugh Gallen	1979-1983
Onslow Stearns	1869-1871	John H. Sununu	1983-1989
James A. Weston	1871-1872	Judd Gregg	1989-
Ezekiel Straw	1872-1874		
James A. Weston	1874-1875		
Person C. Cheney	1875-1877		

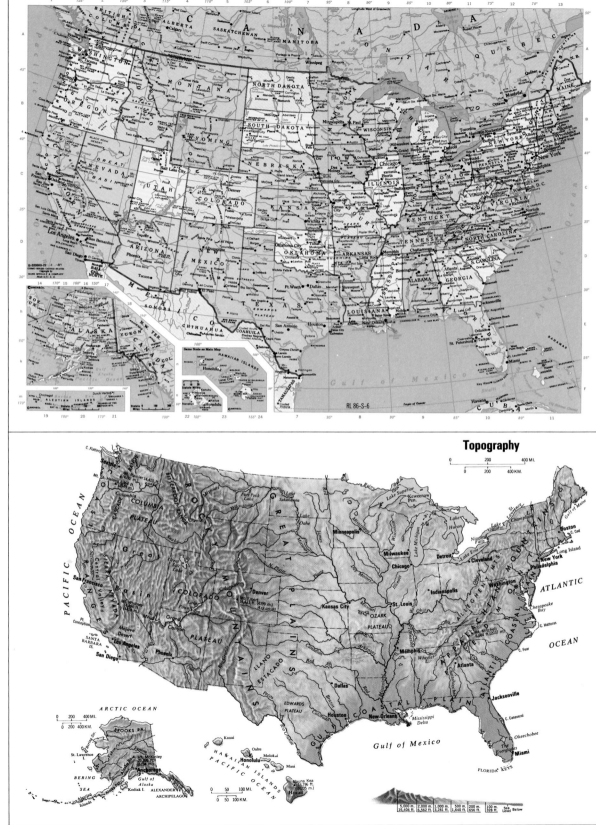

Topography

Jaffrey E2
Jaffrey Center E2
Jefferson B4
Kearsarge B4
Kellyville D2
Kenne E2
Kensington E5
Kingston E4
Laconia C4
Lancaster B3
Langdon D2
Lebanon C2
Lempster D2
Lincoln B3
Lisbon B3
Little Boars Head E5
Littleton B3
Lochmere D3
Londonderry E4
Loudon D4
Lyme C2
Lyme Center C2
MacDowell Reservoir E2
Mad River C3
Madison C4
Mahoosuc Range B4
Manchester E4
Marlborough E2
Marlow D2
Mascoma Lake C2
Mascoma River C2
Mason E3
Melvin Village C4
Meredith C3
Meredith Center C3
Meriden C2
Merrimack E4
Merrimack River D3
Merrymeeting Lake D4
Middleton D4
Milan A4
Milford E3
Millville Lake E4
Milton D5
Milton Mills D5
Mirror Lake C4
Mohawk River g7
Monadnock, Mount E2
Monroe B2
Moore Reservoir B3
Moose River B4
Moriah , Mount B4
Moultonboro C4
Mount Sunapee D2
Mount Vernon E3
Munsonville D2
Nashua E4
Nashua River E3
Nelson E2
New Boston E3
New Castle D5
New Durham D4
New Hampton C3
New Ipswich E3
New London D3
Newbury D2
Newfields D5
Newfound Lake C3
Newmarket D5
Newport D2
Newton E4
Newton Junction E4
Noone E3
North Branch D3
North Chichester D4
North Conway B4
North Hampton E5
North Haverhill B2
North Newport D2
North Pelham E4
North Salem C3
North Sanbornton C3
North Sandwich C4
North Stratford A3
North Sutton D3
North Swanzey E2
North Walpole D2
North Woodstock B3
Northfield D3
Northwood Center D4
Northwood Ridge D4
Nottingham D4
Orford C2
Orfordville C2
Ossipee C4
Ossipee Lake C4
Ossipee Mountains C4
Otter Brook E2
Otter Brook Lake, reservoir E2
Passaconaway, Mount C4
Pawtuckaway Pond D4
Peabody River B4
Pelham E4
Pemigewasset River C3
Peterborough E3
Piermont C2
Pike B2
Pilot Range A4
Pinardville E3
Pine River C4
Pine Valley E3
Pinkham Notch, pass B4
Piscataqua River D5
Piscataquog River D3
Pittsburg f7
Pittsfield D4
Plainfield C2
Plaistow E4
Pleasant Lake D4
Pliny Range B4

Plymouth C3
Portsmouth D5
Potter Place D3
Presidential Range B4
Randolph B4
Raymond D4
Redstone B4
Rindge E2
Rochester D5
Rumney C3
Rumney Depot C3
Rye D5
Rye Beach E5
Saco River B4
Salem E4
Salisbury D3
Salisbury Heights D3
Salmon Falls River D5
Sanbornton D3
Sanbornville C4
Sandown E4
Sandwich C4
Sandwich Range C3
Seabrook E5
Second Lake f7
Severance D4
Silver Lake C4, E2
Silver Lake C4
Somersworth D5
Soucook River D4
Souhegan River E3
South Acworth D2
South Barnstead D4
South Chatham B4
South Danville E4
South Hooksett D4
South Lyndeboro E3
South Merrimack E3
South Sutton D3
South Wolfeboro C4
Spofford E2
Spofford Lake E2
Squam Lake C4
Squam Mountains C3
Stark A4
Stearns Brook A4
Stewartstown f6
Stoddard D2
Strafford D4
Stratford A3
Stratham D5
Sugar Hill B3
Sugar River D2
Sugarloaf Mountain A4
Sunapee D2
Sunapee Lake D2
Sunapee Mountain D2
Suncook D4
Suncook Lakes D4
Suncook River D4
Surry Mountain Lake, reservoir D2
Sutton D3
Swanzey Center E2
Swift Diamond River g7
Swift River B4
Tamworth C4
Tecumseh, Mount C3
Temple E3
Tilton D3
Troy E2
Twin Mountain B3
Umbagog Lake A4
Union D4
Wallis Sands D5
Walpole D2
Warner D3
Warner River D3
Warren C3
Washington, Mount B4
Washington D2
Waukewan, Lake C3
Weare D3
Wendell D2
Wentworth C3
Wentworth Lake C4
West Alton C4
West Brentwood E4
West Campton C2
West Canaan C2
West Chesterfield E1
West Epping D4
West Nottingham D4
West Ossipee C4
West Peterborough E3
West Rindge E2
West Rumney C3
West Rye E5
West Stewartstown g6
West Swanzey E2
West Thornton C3
West Wilton E3
Westmoreland E2
Westport E2
Westville E4
White Mountains B3
Whitefield B3
Wild River B4
Wilmot Flat D3
Wilton E3
Wilton Center E3
Winchester E2
Windham E4
Winnipesaukee C4
Winnipesaukee Lake C4
Winnisquam C3
Winnisquam Lake C3
Wolfeboro C4
Wolfeboro Falls C4
Woodstock C3
Woodsville B2

MAP KEY

Adams, Mount B4
Alexandria C3
Alstead D2
Alstead Center D2
Alton D4
Alton Bay D4
Amherst E3
Ammonoosuc River B3
Andover D3
Androscoggin River A4
Antrim D3
Ashland C3
Ashuelot E2
Ashuelot River E2
Atkinson E4
Auburn D4
Baboosic Lake E3
Baker River C3
Barlett B4
Barnstead D4
Barrington D4
Bath B3
Beaver Brook E4
Bedford E3
Belmont D4
Bennington D3
Berlin B4
Bethlehem B3
Blackwater Reservoir D3
Blackwater River D3
Blue Hills Range D4
Boscawen D3
Bow D3
Bow Lake D4
Bradford D3
Brentwood E4
Bretton Woods B4
Bridgewater C3
Bristol C3
Brookline E3
Cabot, Mount A4
Campton C3
Canaan C2
Canaan Center C2
Canaan Street C2
Candia D4
Candia Village D4
Canobie Lake E4
Canterbury D3
Cascade B4
Center Barnstead D4
Center Conway C4
Center Effingham C4
Center Harbor C4
Center Ossipee C4
Center Sandwich C4
Center Strafford D4
Center Tuftonboro C4
Charlestown D2
Chesham E2
Chester E4
Chesterfield E2
Chichester D4
Chocorua C4
Chocorua, Mount C4
Claremont D2
Clinton D3
Colebrook g7
Concord D3
Connecticut River D2
Conway C4
Conway Lake C4
Cornish Flat C2
Crawford Notch, pass B4
Crescent Range B4
Croydon D2
Crystal Lake D4
Danbury C3
Danville E4
Dead Diamond River g7
Deerfield D4
Derry E4
Dixville Notch g7
Dixville Notch, pass g7
Dover D5
Drewsville D2
Dublin E2

Dunbarton D3
Durham D5
East Alstead D2
East Andover D3
East Candia D4
East Conway B4
East Derry E4
East Grafton C3
East Hampstead E4
East Haverhill B3
East Holderness C3
East Kingston E5
East Lempster D2
East Rindge E3
East Sullivan E2
East Swanzey E2
East Unity D2
East Wakefield C4
Eisenhower, Mount B4
Ellis River B4
Enfield C2
Enfield Center C2
Epping D4
Epsom D4
Errol A4
Etna C2
Everett Lake D3
Exeter E5
Exeter River E5
Farmington D4
First Connecticut Lake f7
Fitzwilliam E2
Fitzwilliam Depot E2
Francestown E3
Francis Lake f7
Franconia B3
Franconia Notch, pass B3
Franklin D3
Franklin Falls Reservoir C3
Freedom C4
Fremont E4
Gale River B3
Gardner Mountain B2
Georges Mills D2
Gilford C4
Gilmanton Iron Works D4
Gilmanton D4
Gilsum D2
Glen B4
Goffstown D3
Gorham B4
Goshen D2
Gossville D4
Grafton C3
Grantham D2
Greenfield E3
Greenland D5
Greenville E3
Groton C3
Groveton A3
Guild D2
Halls Stream f6
Hampstead E4
Hampton E5
Hampton Beach E5
Hampton Falls E5
Hancock E3
Hanover C2
Harrisville E2
Haverhill B2
Henniker D3
Hill C3
Hillsboro D3
Hillsborough D3
Hillsborough Lower Village D3
Hillsborough Upper Village D3
Hinsdale E2
Holderness C3
Hollis E3
Hooksett D4
Hopkinton D3
Hopkinton Lake D3
Hudson E4
Intervale B4
Island Pond E4
Israel River B3
Jackson B4

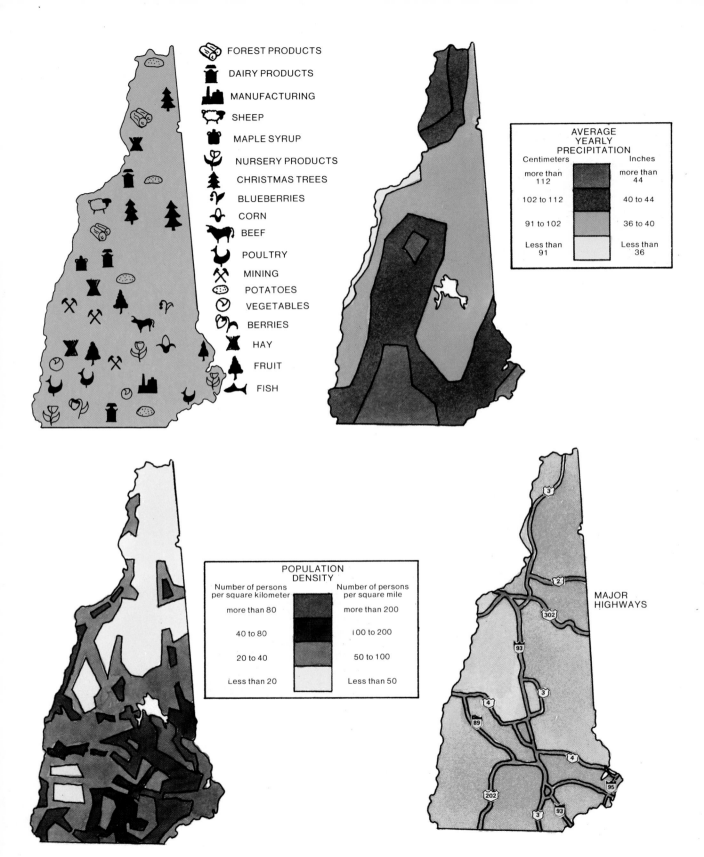

FOREST PRODUCTS
DAIRY PRODUCTS
MANUFACTURING
SHEEP
MAPLE SYRUP
NURSERY PRODUCTS
CHRISTMAS TREES
BLUEBERRIES
CORN
BEEF
POULTRY
MINING
POTATOES
VEGETABLES
BERRIES
HAY
FRUIT
FISH

AVERAGE
YEARLY
PRECIPITATION

Centimeters		Inches
more than 112		more than 44
102 to 112		40 to 44
91 to 102		36 to 40
Less than 91		Less than 36

POPULATION
DENSITY

Number of persons per square kilometer		Number of persons per square mile
more than 80		more than 200
40 to 80		100 to 200
20 to 40		50 to 100
Less than 20		Less than 50

MAJOR
HIGHWAYS

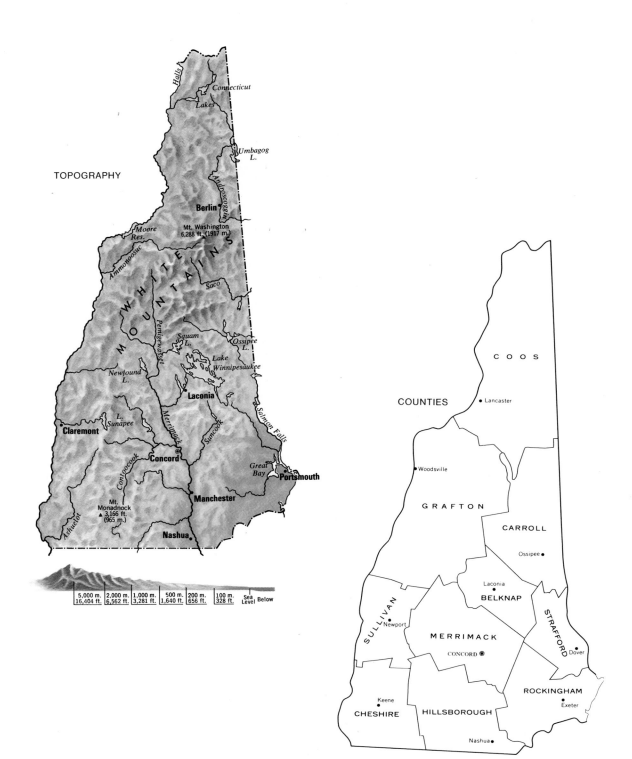

TOPOGRAPHY

Batts

Connecticut

Lakes

Umbagog
L.

Berlin

Moore
Res.

Mt. Washington
6,288 ft. (1917 m.)

Ammonoosuc

W H I T E

M O U N T A I N S

Saco

Pemigewasset

Squam
L.

Ossipee
L.

Lake
Winnipesaukee

Newfound
L.

Laconia

L.
Sunapee

Merrimack

Suncook

Salmon Falls

Claremont

Contoocook

Concord

Great
Bay

Portsmouth

Manchester

Mt.
Monadnock
▲ 3,166 ft.
(965 m.)

Ashuelot

Nashua

| 5,000 m. 16,404 ft. | 2,000 m. 6,562 ft. | 1,000 m. 3,281 ft. | 500 m. 1,640 ft. | 200 m. 656 ft. | 100 m. 328 ft. | Sea Level | Below |

COUNTIES

C O O S

Lancaster

Woodsville

GRAFTON

CARROLL

Ossipee

Laconia

BELKNAP

SULLIVAN

Newport

MERRIMACK

CONCORD ✸

STRAFFORD

Dover

Keene

HILLSBOROUGH

ROCKINGHAM

Exeter

CHESHIRE

Nashua

The Wentworth village green

INDEX

Page numbers that appear in boldface type indicate illustrations

**Sailing on
Lake Sunapee**

Picture Identifications
Front cover: Autumn, Hillsboro Center
Pages 2-3: Young people playing ice hockey on Bradley Lake
Page 6: The Old Man of the Mountain
Pages 8-9: The Swift River near the Kancamagus Highway
Pages 18-19: Montage of New Hampshire residents
Page 26: A nineteenth-century engraving of a harvest scene in New Hampshire
Page 40: New Hampshirites in Revolutionary War dress during Muster Field Days
Page 56: A shoe factory in Derry, about 1880
Page 66: The state capitol in Concord
Pages 78-79: A family canoeing on Squam Lake
Pages 88-89: Harrisville
Page 108: Montage of state symbols, including the state flag, state tree (white birch), state bird (purple finch), state animal (white-tailed deer), state amphibian (red-spotted newt), and state flower (purple lilac)
Back cover: Wild lupines near Sugar Hill in the White Mountains

About the Author

Sylvia McNair writes books and articles about interesting places for adults and young people. A graduate of Oberlin College, she has toured all fifty of the United States and more than thirty foreign countries. Sylvia McNair lives in Evanston, Illinois. She has three sons, one daughter, and two grandsons.

Picture Acknowledgments

About the Author

Sylvia McNair writes books and articles about interesting places for adults and young people. A graduate of Oberlin College, she has toured all fifty of the United States and more than thirty foreign countries. Sylvia McNair lives in Evanston, Illinois. She has three sons, one daughter, and two grandsons.